Life of Lisa

OVERCOMING ADVERSITY WITH LOVE AND LAUGHTER

Lisa Marie Heath

Life of Lisa: Overcoming Adversity with Love and Laughter

© 2023 Life of Lisa Inc

All rights reserved. No part of this book may be reproduced in any form without permission in writing from the author. Reviewers may quote brief passages in reviews.

No part of this publication may be reproduced or transmitted in any form or by any means, mechanical or electronic, including photocopying or recording, or by any information storage and retrieval system, or transmitted by email without permission in writing from the author.

Neither the author nor the publisher assumes any responsibility for errors, omissions, or contrary interpretations of the subject matter herein. Any perceived slight of any individual or organization is purely unintentional.

Brand and product names are trademarks or registered trademarks of their respective owners.

To ensure privacy and confidentiality, the names and other identifying characteristics of the persons and places included in this book have been changed. All the personal examples of my own life and experiences have not been altered.

ISBN 978-1-961185-30-2 (hardcover)
ISBN 978-1-961185-31-9 (eBook)

Book editing & layout: Megs Thompson – megswrites llc – www.megswrites.com

www.inomniaparatuspublishing.com

I DEDICATE THIS BOOK TO MY AMAZING PARENTS, JANN & WAYNE.
LOVE YOU MOM & DAD!

THIS BOOK IS FOR THE SURVIVORS WHO'VE PERSEVERED,
TRIUMPHED, STUMBLED, FALLEN, AND GOTTEN BACK UP, AND FOR
THE PEOPLE WHO LOVE US.

Table of Contents

Introduction 1

In The Beginning 5

Chris 17

Cancer x 2 37

You've Gotta Have Faith 53

Limbo 77

Have Faith, Will Travel 85

Crash 93

I Did It 111

Something Was Wrong 119

Hey God, It's Me, Lisa 139

Here We Are Now 161

Epilogue 165

About The Author 167

Introduction

Are you familiar with the story of Job? In case you aren't, allow me to refresh your memory. Once upon a time, a biblical time, there was a super-wealthy man named Job. He lived with his family, which in biblical times meant he had a house full of people, as well as herds, gaggles, and flocks of any number of animals.

Job was a good guy. He took care of his family, loved his wife and children, treated his animals with kindness, and always tipped his waitress.

One afternoon, while God and Satan were chatting over a strong cup of joe, God pointed Job out to Satan. Bragging a bit about how he was such a stand-up guy with a healthy fear of God, and an absolute disgust for evil.

Satan argued that Job was only a fan of God's because he'd been spoiled so much. He challenged that if God gave him the opportunity to poke at Job a bit, he'd change his tune and curse God in no time!

God agreed to the challenge, with the stipulation that while Satan could do what he liked to make Job's life a living hell, he could not under any circumstances, actually kill him.

Well, Satan got started right away, and over the course of a single day Job started getting messages from his posse letting him know that his sheep, servants, and TEN of his children had died. The news only got worse when he found out that parts of his home had burned to the ground and a bunch of donkeys were stolen by masked bandits.

As you can imagine, Job freaked out. He started tearing at his clothes, pulling out his hair, and ugly crying. But he also prayed to God, sharing his struggles and heartache.

Satan watched all of this with shock and awe, but he refused to give up.

The next day, Job woke up screaming in pain. During the night his entire body had become covered with infected, seeping, puss-filled boils, and sores. When Job's wife caught sight of her husband's rotting form, she urged him to denounce God, give up, and just die already.

After all, their marital bed was now covered with filth, and would basically need to be burned.

But, despite the pain, Job refused to give up, or turn on God. He held strong to his faith that God had a plan for him, no matter how much life sucked at the moment.

Hearing his screams, three of Job's buddies rushed to the house, desperate to see what all the drama and commotion were about. Their presence seemed to ease his outbursts a bit, and they decided to hang out with him for the next week, keeping a silent vigil while they watched their friend writhe in pain.

After 7 days, Job broke the super-awkward silence, waking his buddies with screams about how he wished he'd never been born! His friends were relieved to see that Job was still alive, but also that he seemed to have come to his senses. They whispered to him about how he'd obviously done something really bad, to cause his life to suck so badly, and urged him to ask God for forgiveness for his terrible wrongdoings. They went on to tell Job that his kids had definitely brought their deaths on themselves, with sins of their own.

Job, usually a very patient and kind man, flipped out on his friends. He yelled at them, and God, demanding to know why he was being judged for his supposed deeds when God is in charge of things. Why the hell didn't God just stop Job and his children from making the mistakes that sentenced him to his current hellish situation, and his children to death?!

Job went on to question aloud how it is that a person can ever hope to meet God's expectations, turning into a bitter, anxious, angry, and scared man who despised the fact that God would let evil and bad people thrive, while he, a man who tried his best to be good and honest, had to suffer.

Satan recognized that no matter how unbelievably difficult, painful, disgusting, or depressing he made Job's life, he never truly lost faith in God. And, recognizing that their challenge had run its course, God appeared to Job and commanded that he be brave and remain faithful.

God also got rid of his nasty rash, gave him a shit-ton of new property, a bunch of new kids, and a long enough life to see his grandchildren start their own families.

You may be wondering why I've started a book about me, with a story about someone else. Someone who's been dead for a really long time.

I've lost count of how many times my dad has called me Job. Not as a joke, a jab, or to diminish how I may be feeling, but as a not-so-gentle reminder that the key is always to keep going. Never give up. Never give in. And always, always, always, maintain faith.

So, that was Job's story. It's about time I start telling you mine.

In The Beginning

Unlike the story of Job, the Bible left out the part of how Job came about his faith. Which from my understanding is nothing compared to his later years in life. However, I want to share the story of how I came about my faith here. This is how my story starts.

I want to take you back in time, not as far back as biblical times, a little over 30-some years back is all. It was a cold sunny day in Jacksonville, Florida. I'm guessing here, it may have been raining, but what would I know it's Florida's bipolar season of hot, cold, and rainy. On Tuesday, November 11, I was born. At this point, I'm sure my eyes weren't even open, but what I do know is that my parents were about to get the call they'd been waiting for, for over 10 years. That past Saturday my mother and father had Chinese food at a little family restaurant. When Mom selected hers from the little dish of fortune cookies the waitress brought at the end of their meal, it read, *"You will be given a very special present on Tuesday."* Can you guess what the gift was? Yep, it was me! At the time, none of us could have predicted what God had planned.

I was playing in my room sometime in the year 1993. I remember sitting there with the light shining in through the window and onto the floor. My parents walked in, sat down on either side of me, and just looked at me for what felt like minutes, even though it was probably no more than a few seconds. I thought I was in trouble. You know those serious sit-down conversations that usually mean you've done something wrong? While I was relieved to not be in trouble, I had no way of knowing that my world was about to be rocked in a way that left me spinning for well over 2 decades. I don't remember exactly what words my mom used, nor did I really understand. The short story was, I was adopted!!!!

MY PARENTS WEREN'T MY REAL PARENTS!!!!!

I was only 8 years old and confused, to say the least. But I mean come on, how is an 8-year-old supposed to process that kind of news? I don't blame my parents for what they did, they had no way of knowing when the "right time" was, to tell their child that she was adopted. Remember, this was way before Google or AskJeeves. Looking back now, I bet the entire situation was pretty scary on their end too. But at that moment I felt lost and confused, with no idea who the heck I was.

My mom is one of the greatest angels on God's green Earth. She did her absolute best to explain how sometimes people aren't able to have their own children, and God always has a plan for all of his children. *"He chose us to be your parents. No matter what."* I know that at the time she was trying to be comforting, but I was 8 years old and NOT having it. I no longer knew who I was. Like seriously, do I even have real parents?? The folks I lived with were imposters who'd been lying to me for my entire life. Dude, I watched *Poltergeist* and *Gremlins*, I know what can happen.

And, if I wasn't part of this family, who was I? The rest of that day played out like a huge tantrum, as you might imagine. I told my parents to get out of my room and yelled after them that I was never, ever, ever, ever coming out! I curled up on my bed with my cat, Midnight, and cried. We, Midnight and I, stayed in my room for the next couple of days, only slipping out when "nature called." I'm sure my mother had to write a note when I finally went back to school. *"Please excuse Lisa's absence from school, she has been home sick with the flu."* Mom, the angel that she is, left food outside my door every day, knocking softly to ask if I was okay. *Side note: This entire experience and situation are one of the primary reasons why I dislike being asked, "Are you okay," to this day.*

While my father may be the person who led me back to the Book of Job, my mom is the one who has the patience of Job, especially when it comes to my dad and me. Over the course of that year, I started attending church services with my grandmother. When the weather was nice, we would walk the quick block and a half down the road, it became our special thing, and before too long I chose to be baptized. My grandmother knew that I was searching for something to hold on to. Trying desperately to figure things out. To figure out my life with no real family. *"Really, who am I?"* That single question has continued to play a huge role in my life. I had no idea of what my family history might have been, I really didn't know a damned thing, other than that I was nobody. I could have sworn with all my heart that I had my father's blood in me. That whole nature vs nurture debate though, honestly, if you didn't know any better, you'd believe I was their kid. My height is between theirs and we genuinely look like we're related. Plus, I act so much like my father, that the saying "like father like daughter" could have been written about us. We're two strong-willed peas in a pod, and while it hasn't always been that way, we've both definitely grown past those "rough" times, thank God. Faith has played a huge role in my life, while I was growing up and to this day.

Throughout the years with every school project or assignment, my list of questions grew and grew until my curiosity finally got the better of me. In undergraduate school, I realized that I had an opportunity to write an undergrad thesis and I did just that. I found a mentor and headed out on a journey of investigation and self-discovery. The experience did help answer some of my questions, though it definitely didn't cover them all.

Fast forward to grad school. I was studying Clinical Mental Health Counseling, and during that first year, it was suggested, well "strongly recommended," that if anyone in the program had any unresolved issues in their lives, now was a good time to deal with them. Because if we didn't handle them now, they could become triggers in future sessions with clients. My biological mother was definitely an unresolved issue in my life. I'd thought that I'd moved on, but those questions and my curiosity were still alive and well, which meant I had to deal with them once and for all. (*God, why'd you have to make me such a curious cat?!*) Asking my parents was out of the question because I didn't want them to know what I was doing. Looking at the papers I'd been given when I turned 18 gave me only the most basic idea of who my biological parents were, as well as a partial medical history of my family from when I was adopted back in the 80s. Thank God Mom decided to wait until after I graduated from high school before she shared that paperwork with me. That's when I first saw the information about the adoption agency that had handled my placement.

Back to my original point, clearing up my own personal unresolved issues, to better help my future clients, and avoid any poorly timed triggers. When I contacted the adoption agency, they explained that I would have to pay them to reach out to my birth mother. And just because I wrote her a letter, didn't mean I would ever hear back. It was her choice if she ever wanted to reach back out or have a conversation with me. I paid $100 in hopes that she'd respond but was also pretty sure that she wouldn't want anything to do with me. I remember it took over a month for the adoption agency to serve as the buffer/messenger between us, delivering my letters to her, and vice versa. I really only wanted to collect some details about my birth father, his medical history, as well as her own. I had dealt with serious health issues in the past and was hoping for a little insight into my biological medical history. I thought that was only fair. The other big thing that only Stephanie (my bio mother) could tell me, was who my birth father actually was. Like are you kidding me, in the whole wide world she's the only person that has that info? I highly doubt that, but what the flock! And, because it was completely her choice if she wanted to write back and communicate with me or not, things really were in God's hands.

I started my first letter to Stephanie with some small talk about my life but moved quickly into the few questions I had. I wrote that I hoped she'd be able to provide me with any updated medical history for both her side and my birth father's (remember, the last info I had was as of the '80s when I was born). I asked that she provide me with my biological father's name, as well as where he was buried, and any other information she could share to help shed light on the missing pieces of my life. Well, you won't believe what happened next. Seriously, I couldn't make this shit up, even if I tried. Stephanie did write back, with loopy and bubbly handwriting, with colorful pens, and sparkles. Think high school, using your favorite glitter pen to pass your best friend a note about the boy you like. Right away I asked myself, why did I even try? While reading her letter I kept wondering, when is she going to actually answer my questions? The answer was, not in this letter. Instead, she focused on herself, her life, and how she was doing. NOT what I'd paid to hear about. I was flocking pissed. Seriously, what the actual flock!? Sitting in disbelief next to my then-boyfriend a memory of a situation from my preteens came rushing back. Before this letter, I knew very little about my biological father, only that he'd passed away before I was born. That was a revelation I received from Mom on Mother's Day when I was around the age of 10. Oops, I really flocked up that day. Mom 1 - Lisa 0. LOL But that's a story in itself.

One of the other reasons I was pissed off was that when I read her letter, I realized my birth mother was truly out of her flocking mind. Why did I think that? WELL, the adoption agency my parents used actually called my house. I didn't know who was on the other end of the phone when I answered it, (this was way before Caller ID was invented) but the woman on the other end knew who I was.

"Is this Lisa?"

"Umm yea."

"Is your mother there?"

"Yesss…"

I handed the receiver to Mom and stood there watching (and listening) while she spoke to the strange lady on the phone, dying to know what was being said. Mom kept giving me the "mom finger," You know the one that means hold on, wait a minute, and shut up, all at the same time. It wasn't a long conversation and when she hung up, Mom looked dumbfounded.

"Who was that, Mom? She knew my name."

"They were calling to give us an update on your birth Mother."

"Who's they? What kind of update?"

"Well, I guess your birth mother called the adoption agency recently, to ask how many children she'd given up."

"WHAT????? Mom, how is that even possible?"

I was stunned. What does someone do with that type of information? In times like these my mind runs in many different directions, asking as many questions as I can in hopes of understanding.

"Did she hit her head? How could she forget having babies?"

"Lisa, I have no idea how she forgot or if she hit her head. I'm sorry Lisa, they didn't tell me much."

I've always said that God is the only one who can judge us, and I believe that wholeheartedly. Stephanie, my biological mother, did the best she could for both of us when she chose a better option for me. I'll forever be grateful that I was hand-chosen to be a Heath. I decided at that moment I was going to have to be blunt and to the point in my next letter. No more of this hem-hawing around and being polite. This brings us to the final letter I wrote to Stephanie. I laid out all my cards and held nothing back. Thank God my boyfriend edited things before we actually mailed it. This letter was much shorter than my others. I asked only for my birth father's name, where he was buried, and how he'd passed. That's it. Truthfully, I wanted to know all about him. What was he like? Was he funny? Serious? Creative? I knew that he'd died in a car accident 6 months before I was born. But I'd never know if he had wanted to keep me, to raise me as his daughter, because he never had the chance to make that choice. Which is another story entirely.

Now, let me be clear on something. I never actually planned on contacting my birth father's family. The thought of showing up in their lives years later, when they may not have even known about me to begin with. Heck no! There's no way I was doing that to an elderly couple who'd already lost their son at a young age, with so much life ahead of him. Hence, I had to ask Stephanie for help. After sending that last letter, I basically gave up ever knowing anything about her part of my history. Then, I got a response. I opened her letter and felt like I was reading something I'd written back when I was a pissed-off, angsty teenager. Kind of funny looking back now. She started by telling me how she hoped that the details she provided would help me heal. Followed by my biological father's name, plot number, and which section of the cemetery he was laid to rest in. Then, she included a line of big bold letters that told me everything I needed to know about her.

"YOU WERE NOT A ONE-NIGHT STAND."

I was at a loss for words, which seriously never happens. Like never. Just ask my friends. Really? That's what you decided to put in a letter to your biological daughter? Thanks for sharing, Stephanie, we can totally tell you are in fact not a mom. Knowing that she'd almost lost me after my birth father's life was taken. Requiring her to make serious efforts to ensure I was born a healthy baby. For real lady. You ended our communication like that?! Okay. Whatever. Those were the last words I would ever read or hear about her.

It's funny, I still have those letters from Stephanie somewhere, although I couldn't tell you where, or what other nonsense she'd decided to include. Not even sure why. The next day I skipped classes and headed straight to the cemetery. Off to visit my birth father's grave site. I was overly excited to find out more. It could possibly lead to a future research thesis. LOL All Ph.D. candidates are required to create their own. Anyway, knowing even the tiniest piece of who my biological father was felt like a silver lining at the end of a never-ending day. While driving to the section Stephanie's letter had mentioned, the area started to look familiar, and I realized that I already knew this cemetery really well. It's where my fiancé is buried. No shit. Gotta love the life of Lisa.

GOD LOOKED ACROSS THE TABLE AT SATAN AND SETTING DOWN HIS GRANDE QUAD-SHOT AMERICANO HE ASKED, "WELL, HAVE YOU EVER THOUGHT ABOUT MY BOY JOB? HE'S A REAL MANS-MAN, TAKES CARE OF HIS FAMILY, ALWAYS GETS TO WORK ON TIME, IS A STRAIGHT SHOOTER, A HUGE ANIMAL LOVER, AND HAS A HEALTHY BALANCE OF LOVE & FEAR FOR ME."

Job 2:3 LOLV

Lisa Marie Heath

Chris

A cliff hanger really? Why not? You would've kept reading anyway, right? I mean, hope so. I definitely didn't spend months writing this book for you not to finish reading it.

Anyway, where were we? Oh yea, back to the cemetery, and to answer your question, yes, both my birth father and forever fiancé are laid to rest in the same place, only a few yards away from each other. Like 3,000 steps to be exact.

I've spent hours sitting on my front porch, trying to figure out how to write this chapter. How to capture all of my crazy emotions and feelings into words on a page. But, here goes nothing, and we'll see if any of this actually makes it past my editor and into the book.

Before I can tell you about my fiancé, I need to tell you how we first met.

A long, long time ago, before Facebook there was another online world called Myspace. Anyone who was hip and cool had a Myspace page and AOL chats (which we all got free because of the CD's that were mailed out at least every other month). Internet dating wasn't a thing, and you definitely didn't meet up with strangers at random places. We were babies of the 80's and had been reminded daily by our parents, "stranger danger!"

You may be wondering, *"Why are you explaining this?"* Well, I've never been a great rule-follower, and loved pushing boundaries. So, after chatting with a guy on Myspace for a few days, I decided to meet up with him in person. Or IRL as the kids are saying these days. I showed up at the designated time and place, and Brett showed up with a tag along buddy, Chris.

I was kind of a smart ass, teasing him that he was too scared to meet a girl alone, which broke the ice and left us all laughing. The three of us bowled a few games before heading our separate ways for the night. And that was it. From that night forward, Brett and I were a couple. I've got to tell you though, in hindsight, he was a real son of a you know what.

Brett was the kind of guy that didn't even try to stop his friends from playing jokes on me, yanking me around, or walking all over me. Of course, I wouldn't realize all of that for at least 6-8 months. While we were dating Brett and his bros put me through hell to the point where it felt like I was going through boot camp. The entire time this was happening, that tag along buddy, Chris, was the only person from their group that had my back. Brett and I quickly broke up, but Chris and I remained friends. Like really good friends. I still wonder how Chris and Brett's friendship worked because of how drastically different they were from each other.

Chris was an amazing sounding board, a shoulder to cry on, and one of the most compassionate people I've ever had the pleasure of meeting. He was wise beyond his years and quickly became my best friend. Our love was pure, and we knew almost everything about each other. Chris was the guy who came to my rescue when my car broke down. The person I ran to when I thought I might be pregnant. The man who told me, he didn't care whose baby it was. That if I was pregnant, he'd stand beside me, and we'd parent the child as a team. Chris was the person I called anytime I was in pain. No matter what time zone he was in, or what he was doing, whether that be hanging out with friends or even once, out on a date, he always answered my calls. Chris is the man I continue to visit to share my struggles and successes from a picnic blanket I spread over his final resting place.

Now, before I tell you about our crazy wedding clause, let me tell you what Chris did about a year into our friendship. This son of a you know what joined the Marines without telling me! His mother was the one who called to ask for my address to give to Chris for while he was away for basic training. Boy did I want to KILL him. This seems to be a trend in my life, one that I really don't enjoy. People hide really big things only to tell me about them once they're already done. Maybe it's because they know I'll try everything I can to talk them out of their crazy decisions. Who knows. Brett did the same thing when he went off to boot camp, which I only found out about because his brother hit me up to pass along Brett's new address.

The boys pulled these stunts about a year apart, and when Chris graduated from boot camp and came home, I bitched him out pretty bad for doing the same thing Brett had done previously. I warned him that if he ever did something like that again, he may not survive to see his first duty station. We spent as much time together as we could before he had to leave, and luckily his first duty station was in Pensacola, which was close enough that I still got to see him on a pretty regular basis. Chris was the one who gave me the nickname, Crazy Psycho Bitch, but I couldn't argue with him, it was fitting, and I knew he meant it out of love.

While Chris's days were filled with hours of work and training, he still answered every time I called, at all hours, to complain about college and the pain that lived in my pelvic area. At this point in my medical journey, that pain had become unbearable. While he was stationed in Pensacola, Chris was able to take leave and while he was home, he ended up getting into a pretty gnarly motorcycle crash, which again, I didn't hear about until later. Why am I telling you this? Well, you remember my nickname, right?! While he was being driven to the hospital Chris had managed to instruct that no one dare call me until the following day. When I finally got the call, I rushed to the hospital, but had no way of knowing what I was going to find when I got there. My best friend was lying in the hospital bed, his right leg completely covered with road rash. If he hadn't been wearing his helmet, he would have died.

After Chris was released from the hospital, he stayed with his mom in Jacksonville, and I visited him every chance I had. I was working and going to school at the time, so would often be slipping into the house at ungodly hours, only to check on him, grab a few minutes of sleep, and sneak back out in time for work or class. As he healed, our relationship grew stronger. We were the best of friends and had undeniable love for each other.

Chris wanted to take advantage of all the military benefits available, and proposed to all of his female friends, hoping one of them would say yes. He asked me multiple times if I would marry him, taking our relationship to a different 'friends with benefits' level. I declined every time. Sure, I loved him with my entire heart, but Chris was my best friend, my lifeline, and I never wanted to chance ruining the relationship we had. I was scared that if we were to get married, our relationship dynamic would change, and I might lose him completely. Losing people was kind of a 'thing' in my life starting when I was only 5 years old. Funny side note - as I'm writing this, I'm wearing a shirt that was a staple on the show One Tree Hill. *"People always leave."* What can I say, the evil in the world allows God to use our experiences for the good of others.

Anyway, my medical issues were getting more and more serious, and I was told that there was a pretty strong chance that it was the dreaded C word. Cancer. I called Chris as soon as I got the news and asked if he'd been serious, all those times he'd proposed. He confirmed that he was and wanted to know what happened to make me change my mind. Trust me, that isn't something that happens often or easily. I told him that the doctors thought I could have cancer and had scheduled an appointment with an oncologist. I was in shock about what I was supposed to do next. I mean, what the flock?! I was in my first year of junior college, moving forward in life, debilitating pain in tow. I can't tell you the exact moment Chris and I decided to get married, but we did. Chris had only one requirement, we had to have sex on our wedding night. Talk about changing the dynamic of our relationship.

During this time, Chris was moved from Pensacola to San Diego, and I quickly developed a love hate relationship with the distance. Being so far apart definitely sucked, but the time difference helped us remain connected surprisingly. He adjusted to his new area well, and I did my best to keep a smile on my face through the pain I was experiencing. At the time, I was working as a supervisor for a worldwide corporate gym. One afternoon I happened to find a nice wedding band set someone had forgotten. I called and spoke to the women who I thought they belonged to and was told that they definitely weren't hers. I put them in our safe with a note of the day and place where I found them, and honestly didn't give them another thought until a few months later when my boss brought them up. She let me know that because they'd been in the safe, unclaimed, for over six months, I could have them if I wanted. Since I'd been the one who found them in the first place. I only hesitated for a moment but when I saw that it was a past, present and future style ring, I told her that I'd definitely take the engagement ring off her hands. I raced outside, to the back of the building, and called Chris.

"Chris!"

"Yes Lisa?"

"I have an engagement ring!"

Crickets.

"You have a what?"

"An engagement ring. Now you don't have to worry about getting me one. We will need to get it sized though."

"Wait. What?!"

"Slacker. I've got a damned ring. We're getting married right?"

"Yes, ma'am we are."

"Well, then I need a ring to wear. Duh!"

Chris was dating someone else in San Diego at the time, but it didn't bother me. We'd agreed that we could both continue dating up until we got married and made it official. He was honest and up front with the gal he was seeing, at least I think he was, doesn't really make a difference now. And I did the same with anyone I went out with. We were set to get married in November. Sometime between the 10th and 12th to be exact. The Marines host their annual ball on November 10th, the US Military's birthday, and my birthday is the 11th, so we knew it would be an easy date to remember. No one knew what we were planning except Chris's parents. His mom was a notary and volunteered to be our witness. I bet you're wondering why I hadn't told or invited my parents? Well, they'd always said that if I ever did get married, they'd love it if I would elope, because that's just so much easier than a big fancy wedding. So, I was respecting their wishes, kind of.

Our relationship was in the process of changing. We were transitioning from best friends to husband and wife. Neither of us had any hesitation about saying "I do." We already knew everything we needed to about each other, our family dynamics, and any skeletons hiding in our closets. We didn't have every little detail planned out, but we had enough in place that I was getting butterflies about this huge life changing moment.

But I never got that chance. The Lord decided he was ready for Chris on August 8th, only 3 months before our wedding. My heart still breaks every year on the anniversary of the day I lost him.

When Chris died, I didn't find out from the military or his parents. Remember when I said that I met Chris through his best friend Brett? Well, Brett was the one who called to tell me what happened. He was also the furthest away from me, stationed overseas at the time, but none of this surprises me, I know Chris had a hand in how things played out.

It was 1:30 am when my phone started ringing. I answered it, like I always did, no matter the time of day. The first thing Brett said was that we needed to talk. He knew that I was living with my parents at the time and wasn't sure exactly how I was going to react to the news, so he asked me to go outside and sit down.

"Skeeter's gone Lisa."

"Of course, he's gone. He's in California living it up."

"No Lisa. Skeeter's gone. He's dead. I'm calling you because no one else has been able to get ahold of you."

I made a sound that the whole world could feel. I scream-cried and fell to the ground with a thud that broke my heart in half. Brett knew how I processed things and let me have the time I needed to release my pain to the world. With tears streaming down my face, I was finally able to compose myself enough to talk with Brett.

"Please tell me it's not true?"

"Lisa, it breaks my heart but it's the God's honest truth. I'm a wreck too. And I won't be able to make it back to his funeral. There's just nothing I can do over here in this flocking sand-trapped country."

"Brett, are you going to be okay?"

"I'm not 100% sure."

"Fair. Well, at least now I don't have to worry about you over there. Not that I should give a shit about you anyway."

"Thanks Lisa."

"I mean it Brett. Your best friend/brother is in heaven protecting your ass, punk. You're going to be fine."

That was the first of many silver linings I would recognize throughout my life. Those silver-linings have saved my ass from going mentally insane. They're a way for me to see a light at the end of the tunnel when everything seemed to be going wrong.

Brett and I chatted a little more before he had to go. I told him to keep in touch and that I would do the same to relay any information I received. I played *nice* with this man who'd treated me like shit and told him that if he needed a friend or someone to talk to, he knew where to find me.

Now that I was fully awake and trying to process what was happening, God was about to get an earful. I screamed at the top of my lungs, knowing that he could hear me, and praying that he'd answer my cries. But also knowing that God answers in his own time, the right time.

"WTF! WHY?! WHY ME?"

"REALLY? AGAIN?"

"WHAT, YOU DON'T THINK I'VE SUFFERED ENOUGH?"

"THERE'S NO ONE ELSE YOU CAN FLOCK WITH FOR A CHANGE?!"

"NO, LET'S JUST RUIN LISA'S LIFE SOME MORE!"

"SERIOUSLY GOD, WHAT DID I DO?"

"SO FAR ITS 3-0 WITH EVIL COMING OUT AHEAD!"

"I'VE LOST EVERYTHING THAT I WAS PROMISED..."

"I SURE AS HELL HOPE YOU AND THE DEVIL ARE HAVING FUN..."

"I'LL JUST BE DOWN HERE, FALLING APART, WAITING FOR ANSWERS..."

Both God and I knew that our personal relationship had changed. It felt like an atomic bomb had exploded between us, with God and I walking away from the damage, headed in different directions. That wasn't the first nor would it be the last time that God and I went head-to-head.

After a night of screaming, crying, and genuinely wanting to die, I got up, got dressed, and drove to work. Getting out of my Toyota Celica I slammed the door so hard that I thought I'd broken my own window. My boss was walking up at the same time and noticed that I definitely wasn't okay.

"Lisa, what's up? You look like you could spit fire."

I snapped my head around to face him and let him know that my birthday vacation was no longer needed. Since my fiancé passed away and you can't get married to dead people.

His jaw dropped and it was obvious that he had absolutely no clue what to say.

"So, Steve today's going to be a completely different day at work. I know you're my boss, but my fiancé passed away and I didn't find out until about 1:30 this morning. I've left a message for his mother to give me a call when she can. She'll be calling my cell phone and when it goes off, I will be walking off the sales floor to take the call in private. I do not know how I'm going to be after that call, so I would recommend you get someone to come in and cover for me. Oh, and I'm not okay, but let's get this shit together and get to work."

Just then, while Steve was still in shock, my cell phone started vibrating and a familiar number ran across my screen. I looked at my boss, he said nothing and just nodded his acceptance. I took the call outside, behind the building, with the door propped open. I sat on the curb, took a deep breath, and answered the phone.

"Okay Momma Nooreen, I'm all yours."

Chris's mom apologized profusely about not having been able to get a hold of me. Her voice was torn, worried, and scared. I knew then that I was going to need to step up and help her with anything I could because Chris wasn't only my fiancé, he was her baby boy. I asked her if we were going to set up a slideshow for his service, showcasing pictures of Chris doing what he loved. She let me know that she hadn't even thought about that but would like it very much. I told her that when I got off work, I would drive over to her house to help with things

When I arrived at Momma Nooreen's house that afternoon, Chris's father George enveloped me in his arms and told me that I would always be his daughter in law. It was a moment I'll never forget, and one that I wish for the life of me, hadn't needed to happen. Once we were able to talk, I would find out how Chris passed away.

That's when I knew that all the deep feelings Chris and I had for each other would have turned into a truly amazing love between us. When I woke up the next morning, I knew what I had to do. I got dressed and headed to the local mall where a family friend worked at a really nice jewelry store. The moment I walked in the store she rushed to give me a hug. Her hug caused me to break down and cry. We walked over to the jewelry counter. As I was sitting down and wiping the tear away, I saw Teresa pulling another chair closer to mine. I looked at my mother's friend and said, *"I need your help. My best friend Chris passed away. We had a different love."* Teresa asked a question that pierced my heart. *"How did he pass?"* Tears rolled down my cheeks.

"Doing what he loved most, riding his motorcycle. He had been out riding the mountains in San Diego. On the way up the mountain, one set of brakes stopped working. Once at the top, he and his 2 riding partners checked out his bike. After looking it over, they headed back. He was still able to drive it. Honestly, Teresa I know nothing about motorcycles. LOL The plan was to have one rider as the leader, Chris in the middle, with the last rider covering the rear. Weaving around the curves the leader passed a truck, then waived Chris that it was clear. A vehicle came speeding around causing Chris to fly down the mountain and hit the only tree, HEAD on!! He died instantly."

Sobbing I told her, *"I want to buy a wedding band and have it engraved."*

"Of course."

"Great, I needed one in white gold."

Okay, let's look at our collection of bands. I chose a band and asked if it could say, *"RIP Chris C."*

I want him to keep him close to my heart, since we were getting married in a few months. Teresa looked at me and lost it. She'd never had a request like mine. I knew at that moment that I was never going to be that version of Lisa again.

This wasn't how our plan was meant to go. It was a nightmare that I wanted desperately to wake up from but couldn't, no matter how hard I cried, how loud I screamed, or how much I prayed.

It's no question that evil is consistently trying to challenge my perseverance and strength. It hates that I always find a way to overpower it, to overcome the hurdles it places in my path, even if that means sitting in my car sobbing over the loss of my fiancé while thanking God for the time we had together.

Have you ever witnessed a deceased military personnel being flown home to their family? Before this I'd only seen it in movies. I'd never seen the casket, draped with the American flag, being unloaded with care and respect. I didn't think I ever would. This was the first time I had even been to *that* side of the airport. While a bunch of us went to show our support for the family, only a handful of people would be able to go back and witness the arrival of Chris's casket. As his parent's and close family members made their way through the crowd, one of his relatives pushed me to go with them. They said they knew that he would have wanted me there. I was the last one allowed access and with every step I took, it felt as if the world around me was turning into a movie. A set with actors. It didn't seem real. Every time I blinked; I expected the screen to change. My happiness and joy for the world slowly started to slip away. I had finally passed the denial stage and moved on to anger. At least that's what it felt like. I no longer had a heart. I was numb and couldn't feel anything. I wondered if anyone else could recognize the shell of a person I was becoming.

Chris always had a thrill for the theatrics, and passing away didn't seem to stop him. Right after his body had been returned to us, and delivered to the funeral home, the family and I were told that a tropical storm was headed directly our way. I figure Chris just wanted a little bit more time with us, and honestly, the storm was a blessing in disguise. Most of Jacksonville shut down for a few days with very limited business hours and most bridges closed. Yet somehow, I always found a clear way from my house or work to the funeral home, and back again. For almost a week I drove twice a day, through a tropical storm to sit in a room with his casket. I needed Chris to hear what I had to say. Plus, being there with him, was a safe place to scream, cuss, and cry. No one was there to judge me, or how I grieved. The anger that was inside of me felt like the devil trying to tear his way out. And, while I will always trust God above all else, there was evil living inside of me for longer than I'd like to admit. I was constantly fighting an inner battle with myself between the two. Anger, the evil, and acceptance, the good.

When the storm passed, the day finally came. "C-Day." I sat in my car in the parking lot of the funeral home, watching as Chris's eclectic variety of friends poured into the building. From bikers to military personnel, and everyone in between. I'd made it this far but wasn't sure if I could get out of the car, let alone walk inside. I was 5 minutes late for the service and it was standing room only. I remember smiling, amid the pain and grief, seeing the outpouring of love and support, all of the people that Chris had touched, the lives he'd changed. I weaseled my way into the room, past the crowd of people standing outside the front door, and stood against the back wall, next to two of Chris's female friends.

Even though I knew what to expect during the latter half of a military funeral service, witnessing it there, for Chris, was different. It was soul wrenching, and I wasn't sure that I would survive. Military officers lifted the American flag from his casket and folded it with precision, while the bugle played Taps, and the 21-gun salute began. I could feel the pain as every single shot pierced through my heart until I could no longer stand and crumbled onto the shoulder of Chris's friend beside me. She held me close and let me sob all over her, tears, snot, and all. It wasn't my prettiest moment, but she didn't say anything, just let me cry. Once I'd composed myself, I introduced myself to her as one of Chris's friends.

As we all made our way back towards the parking lot someone in the crowd heard my voice and yelled, *"Is that psycho bitch?"* I froze. Then, because these were Chris's people, I turned around and yelled back, *"Yep!"* With tears still running down my face I watched as 3 people broke away from the crowd and made their way towards me. They all knew who I was, and how special I was to Chris. One of them shared, *"When you called Chris, we all knew to be quiet and let him have his time with you."* He had shared with them all about my medical troubles, as well as that the nights were when I experienced the most pain. Which was why the time difference between us worked so well in our favor. While we were talking, I could hear as Chris's motorcycle friends started their bikes to do their own tribute. I still have that video and it never ceases to touch my heart.

While I was still heartbroken and devastated at the loss of my best friend and fiancé, God was amazing through it all. He and Chris made sure to leave me in the open arms of that friend. The one who held me while I cried and listened as I screamed. She became one of my best friends, and a constant part of my life for nearly 15 years.

With Chris gone, I found myself alone, again. My best friend was dead. I felt like I had no one to turn to, and I was scared to death about facing the possibility of Cancer. (Bet you forgot about that little tid-bit.)

With all my might I screamed his full legal name at the sky. (Yep, my 'mom' voice came out.) Remember, we weren't only getting married because we were best friends and loved each other. We both knew that my medical issues were going to be a really big deal and I was going to need really good coverage if I hoped to make it through everything alive. Like I said before, you can't marry a dead person. My world came to a crashing halt. Planning for a wedding and marriage turned into a hunt for medical insurance.

In those moments, I called out to God, praying he would send an answer.

"God, I know I'm strong but why?"

"Why Me?"

"Can't I get a break?"

"I miss my best friend, and I don't know what I'm supposed to do."

"Oh, and one more thing God, can you please give him a hug for me?

WHEN HE HEARD THE DEVASTATING NEWS, JOB FLIPPED OUT. HE STARTED TEARING AT HIS CLOTHES & SHAVED OFF HIS HAIR (BRITTANY-STYLE). BUT THEN, JOB PULLED HIMSELF TOGETHER & DROPPED TO HIS KNEES TO CHAT WITH GOD. "HEY GOD. IT'S ME, JOB. I GET IT, I WAS BORN NAKED & WILL DIE THE SAME. YOU'RE THE BIG-MAN UPSTAIRS, THE GUY IN CHARGE & THE BADASS THAT GAVE ME THE LIFE I HAVE, MY FAMILY, MY HOME, MY HEALTH, HELL, EVERYTHING I HAVE IS FROM YOU. AND, YOU'VE GOT THE POWER TO TAKE IT ALL AWAY. THIS SITUATION SERIOUSLY SUCKS BUT I'M STILL ON TEAM GOD & WILL CONTINUE TO WORSHIP YOU & PRAISE YOUR NAME."

Job 1:20-21   LOLV

Lisa Marie Heath

Cancer x 2

Let me ask a question before diving in. Have you ever felt deep down in your gut that something was off? That without a shadow of doubt, you knew it was true? A feeling deep down in your soul? Yea, me too. I have them all the time actually, and some of them I really wish didn't come true. But, at the end of the day, our gut is always right. Being as headstrong as I am, it's taken quite a while for me to fully trust my gut, but it's never let me down.

Would you believe it if I told you that I've had over 30 surgeries? Yep, you read that right and it's not a typo. 30 - three oh. That's an average of almost 1 surgery per year of my life - wow. Now that's a story. Wanna hear it? Okay, okay. I'm done joking, at least for now. Things are about to get really serious, really fast. I won't bore you with every tiny detail. What I will tell you, is that I'm a medical mystery, thanking the Lord for every day I get. You know those kids in school that got attendance awards for never missing a day? Yea, that was never me and through my high school years it was a miracle that our family didn't kill each other, seriously.

Let's time travel back to my teenage years. Every woman reading this remembers the first time Aunt Flo came to visit. That first week of cramps, frustration, angst, and discomfort. Does anyone else remember that feeling of waddling around school like you were wearing a diaper? No? Just me? Anyway, I'm starting here because my first few years getting to know Aunt Flo were nothing spectacular. It wasn't until high school that she morphed into a full-blown bitch! Freshman year was horrible, I failed Algebra, and while I'd come to realize years later that everyone fails, and it's those failures that allow us to learn, that definitely wasn't the feeling at the time. The year started with me recovering from a knee injury, in and out of the doctor's office and ER (more on this soon), and stuck sitting on the sidelines at dance team practice. My paternal grandmother, the last of my grandparents, passed away, and losing her hit our family like a ton of bricks. While her health was declining mom checked me out of school at least 3 times a week so I could spend as much time as possible at her bedside, and it always seemed to be Algebra that was missed. Well, I mean, I wouldn't exactly say I missed it, but you know what I mean.

I didn't care about missing class, or the threat of failing. The person I cared most about in the world was lying in a bed dying. While I was growing up, she'd always been there for me, treating me differently than she did her kids, other grandkids, and great grandkids. When she passed away, it was a dark period for my father and I. He'd lost his mother, his best-friend, and I'd lost a woman who I knew truly loved me, no if's, and's, or but's. Through all of this, when Aunt Flo arrived each month, I'd become paralyzed with pain. I remember so many times where my mother had to come into my bedroom and actually lift me out of bed because I wasn't able to sit up or move on my own. My stomach hated me - and the feeling was mutual. For an entire week I would cling to a heating pad, taking the strongest pain medication doctors could prescribe, and when that didn't work, off to the ER we went for morphine. I'm not going to sugar coat it, mom and I were making trips to the ER at least once a month, and even then, when we got back home and the morphine wore off, the debilitating pain was right there waiting.

It would have been comical if it wasn't so excruciating. My doctor would send me for laparoscopic surgery after surgery and come back with a different answer about what was going on inside my body every single time. We would leave the hospital with no real answers, and another battle scar as a souvenir. After one such exploration, the doctor explained that the lining of my bladder was disintegrating. What?! How is that even a thing?! By the time he was finished delivering the news all I knew was that I would have to change my entire diet. First you tell me I've got some crazy issue, and now you say I have to give up eating anything I like? At least this time it wasn't gluten. Although, spoiler, that came later.

Through this endless round of appointments, my father accused me of being a hypochondriac, while my mother went full mama bear reminding him that they'd adopted a child (that's me) after 10 long years of waiting, because she couldn't have children herself due to her own struggles with endometriosis. Got to say, I love it when one of my parents gets super protective.

Over the course of 3 years, I was seen by 3 different OBGYN's. Each one conducted countless awkward and uncomfortable ultrasounds looking for cysts hiding on my ovaries. I still don't think they realized how mean the demon in my female organs really was. If you'd have visited our house at this time, you probably would've thought someone had an opiate problem which wasn't the case at all – it was just my medication. The medical cocktail prescribed for me was barely enough to dull the excruciating pain I was dealing with, and even then, the relief was temporary. During this time, Chris and I got really close. He listened when I told him about how I was feeling, what was happening, and how frustrated I was with the lack of answers. He was always a phone call away no matter what time of day or night.

I finally found an OBGYN that believed what I was saying and didn't look at me like I'd sprouted three heads like Medusa. Dr. Brownie ran her tests and blood work, and after reading through my chart, which by this time was as thick as an encyclopedia, she advised that she wanted to refer me to a reproductive specialist. Umm excuse me? I'm in my early 20s and definitely not trying to get pregnant anytime soon. She assured me that while it sounded a little crazy, a reproductive specialist had additional training regarding everything related to the female reproductive system. While I waited a few weeks for my appointment, I was nervous that this new doctor might not take me seriously like Dr. Brownie had. The day of my appointment came and after showing my mom and I back to his office, Dr. Lip sat back and listened to me explain everything.

When I was finished reading the book that was my chart, he looked at me and said, "I believe you." Wait, what? You believe me? I've never heard that before. Dr Lip followed up with his explanation to why. He told me, "Lisa, I'm 99% sure that you've got endometriosis, as well as bilateral hernias." I had NO WORDS. Which rarely happens. Thank God.

Not only did he believe what I was telling him, but he understood what I was saying, and actually thought he knew what might be wrong! I started bawling. He assured me that we'd get things figured out but advised me that he'd also need to check my ovaries for cysts, because a number of them had appeared on a previous ultrasound sent over by Dr Brownie. The last thing he shared with me was that he'd be referring me to another specialist for hernia repairs. Wait, What? Dr Lip told me that there was a chance some of my pain could be stemming from those cysts. Oh, and one more thing, all of these procedures would be completed concurrently. One right after another.

My visit with the hernia specialist, was by far the easiest medical office I'd ever visited up until that point. I found the building easily because it was right behind the hospital where Dr Lip was located. I signed the check in form, took a seat, signed a few necessary documents, and was shown to a room in no time. The nurse took my vitals, and a few seconds later the doctor was introducing himself, explained how surgery would go, and what I could expect for my recovery. That was it. 15 minutes, in and out.

Fast forward to the weekend before surgery. As I was trying to clear my system out, my body became weak and couldn't keep anything down. It was the worst. Pre-operation prep is horrible in the first place, cutting out everything besides a few select liquids from your diet to help when it comes time for them to blow your stomach full of gas, giving them room to work. I not only had to taste that crap once, but I had the pleasure of tasting it again when it came back up. TMI but sorry, it's what happened.

I am not a morning person, and yet most of my surgeries have all been scheduled for before the sun comes up. This one was no different. About 4 am, after a night of not much sleep, I crawled into moms SUV, and dad drove us the 30 minutes to the hospital. My surgery was scheduled for 6:30am which gave us plenty of time to check in, get settled in my pre-op room, and confirm for every doctor that entered the room, exactly what surgery I was having. I swear, robot Lisa came out and I felt like a drone, answer the same questions over and over again.

During this time, the nurses started to notice that my body temperature was rising. Not a good sign. If my temperature got any higher than 100.9, my surgery would have to be rescheduled, and I was not going to let that happen, no matter how I felt afterward. I had been waiting for almost 10 years to get things resolved and I refused to wait another day. I looked at the nurse and stated, *"Get me Ice packs! I am not leaving without this surgery."* Luckily, she did as I asked and came back with a few different ways to help bring my temperature down.

What's funny is that when I was wheeled back to the freezing cold surgical room, I realized that my temperature and fever wouldn't have been an issue at all, if they'd just let me hang out there for a few minutes.

A few hours later, I was semi-awake, and the doctors came in to tell me that everything was a success.

"Woohoo! Is my ovary gone too?"

"No. We were able to fix both hernias, zap away all of the endometriosis, and remove your cysts. While you were under anesthesia, a sample of your left ovary was sent down to a pathologist, to test it for cancer. At this point the results came back inconclusive, so we haven't figured everything out yet, but we'll talk more about that once you've recovered."

The nurses warned my parents that my fever may come back and that's exactly what happened later that day. Mom being a mother was worried and called the medical center in a panic asking what she should do. The crazy nurses recommended that they put a cold washcloth on my head and have me stick my legs in an ice bath. Taking them literally, my mom made me an ice bath, but only for my legs, because of my incisions and stitches. Of course, this was all easier said than done because I couldn't sit up, bend over, or walk by myself, so my parents had to help me sit up, swirl my legs around to the side of the bed, and once my feet touched the floor, grab under my armpits to lift me up. My mom walked beside me, my dad behind me, with both of his arms under my own, and together the three of us walked the 25 steps from my bed to the toilet, where I sat and rested for a minute. My insane mother then told me that she thought I needed to be sitting in the tub filled with water and ice, to which I said, nope! I knew that if I somehow managed to get all the way down into the tub, there was no way we were getting me back up. So, I stood in the flocking freezing water for as long as I could before walking the 25 steps back to my bed. To this day I don't understand how so many people think ice baths are an amazingly healing experience.

While I loved the fact that the specialists were able to address so many issues at once, having both hernias, endometriosis, and ovarian cysts all tackled at the same time was definitely not the best idea. The recovery process took much longer than I'd expected, and I slept off and on for a few weeks. More off than on. I took it as easy as I could and let my body heal. When it came time for my follow up appointment, I asked the doctor if he'd ever figured out what was going on with my ovaries. He responded that they weren't able to make heads or tails of what was happening. As he showed me the images, they'd taken from the operating room, he informed me that he'd never seen an ovary that looked quite like mine. I thought it was a compliment, the pictures were really cool, with bright purple spots, and I'd always known that I was special. It definitely wasn't a compliment though, and the bright purple spots on my ovaries were not a good sign. I was still trying to process what I was seeing when Dr Lip advised that he was referring me to an oncologist. Talk about a shock.

A month later, while I was driving to my oncology appointment, I had a serious chat with God.

"Lord, if this is true, I ask that you protect me in all ways. I know that cancer is a huge possibility, and I'm trying to prepare myself for whatever it is this new specialist is going to say, but I could still really use your support and backup. In your name. Amen."

While I was waiting in the oncologist's office, I saw so many people, some who you could tell were going through treatments, and others that looked like me. Normal, healthy, young, without issues, except that my stomach and reproductive organs were slowly killing me from inside. During my visit Dr Buck introduced himself and let me know that he'd like to do an ultrasound before anything else, to get a better look for himself at what was going on. As soon as the wand hit my ovary I shouted, "that hurt!" It was only 3 weeks after my bilateral hernia surgery, where they'd cleared all of the cysts from my left ovary, and already it was completely covered again. Dr Buck let me know that I was going to need another surgery, this time to remove this demonic organ, aka my left ovary.

After surgery, I would be taking a full year off from my studies at my junior college. Can you guess who recommended that? Stupid doctors.

Samples were shipped off to 5 different universities (we're talking the big ones) in hopes that one of them might know what the hell was wrong with my demonic ovary. One of the major universities was finally able to clarify what was going on, and the answer was that I had cancer. I honestly wasn't too surprised. I'd known all along, and what I really wanted to say was, "told ya so!" But, when you've got cancer, that's not such a great idea, I guess.

It was mesothelioma to be exact. Yep, the cancer that everyone (including myself) assumed could only be developed in the lungs of people who were exposed to asbestos for long periods of time. Not young women trying to start their lives. Right away, I wanted everything removed. The other ovary, my uterus, all of it! That may seem drastic for my age, but it was my body why couldn't I do that? Insurance said no.

I've known since I was 10 that I didn't want to have children. Mom of course always wanted to play the 'what if game.' What if you change your mind? What if you fall in love and want to start a family? What if you wake up one day and KNOW that you want to have a baby? So, I kept my other reproductive goods and proceeded with 2 rounds of intense IVF, for mom's sake. Throughout that process we discovered that my right ovary (the only one I had left) wasn't producing eggs, meaning the IVF treatments I received were double and triple the normal dose, causing me to bloat up and nearly kill a woman who dared to ask me, "when are you due?" IVF was horrible. When it was time to harvest eggs (finally) they were only able to collect 4. For those who aren't well versed in the IVF 411, the average number of eggs harvested during each round of IVF are between 10-20. And I had 4. I decided at that point that enough was enough. No more IVF for this girl.

They cleared me to begin my education career again after only 6 months. I'm still not sure if this was because they believed I was ready, or if they were just that annoyed with my constant barrage of phone calls and messages. This girl is a Scorpio. Dead middle of the zodiac sign. I am 100% that girl.

Once all of that was taken care of, you'd assume I was free and clear. Nope, my appendix 3 months later decided that after all my surgeries it wanted out too. It was huge. Dr Buck quickly took care of that and I'm sure my manager at work was not happy with all the time I needed off. Take your complaints to my body, you think I would wish or want this for my life? Hard pass.

Now that I was cancer free, I was able to live my life with fewer follow up appointments. Flash forward to October of 2018. Remember this.

I'm 32 years old and it's been 9 years since my left ovary had been removed. That fall I was working for my first bank as a call center representative. After working with the bank for 3 months, I started experiencing those familiar stabbing pains again, to the point where I had to spend much of my shift hunched over my desk.

That afternoon I called Dr. Brownie's nurse, Carmel. I had to leave a message and knew it would be at least the next day before they would call me back. I was right. While on lunch the next day, I got a call from the nurse. She asked if I would be able to make it in that afternoon. Flock yea I could. Not caring what my new job had to say, I knew this was serious. I told my manager and she approved for me to leave right away.

Thank God, I prayed the whole way to her office. I knew it was cancer again. It was my first gut feeling when the pain started. Dr. Brownie loved to see me just not under these circumstances. She pushed on my belly, pelvic region, and sent me down to the ultrasound room. There they performed an internal ultrasound. Once that was over, I waited to see my doctor again and when she came in, I could tell on her face what she was going to say.

"Well, you have cysts on your ovary."

"When are we doing surgery?"

"Lisa, I no longer do surgeries."

"What? Since when?"

"A few years ago."

"Okay. Who do you recommend?"

She named a few doctors then said that I should try to get on one of their calendars right away and agreed that she would see me for a follow up appointment when everything was taken care of, again.

She hugged me and we walked out. I made an appointment for 2 days later to see the new doctor and couldn't wait to hear what he suggested. My birth mother had suffered from uterine cancer and while I didn't have nerves about the appointment, I was praying that he would have some ideas to help fix things once and for all. He did not disappoint.

"Lisa, I have reviewed your chart. From what I've read, I would recommend we remove your other ovary. We can

also remove everything while we are in there if that's what you wish."

Without a pause I said, "YES, THAT'S WHAT I WANT! TAKE IT ALL. I am done. I had 4 eggs saved; my best friend is gone, and shoot, I'm one week away from turning 33."

"Are you sure?"

"Yes, I'm sure. I mean, why the fuck would I want to go through all of this for my right ovary, then in a few years do it again for my uterus?"

I told them to just take it out, all of it. And we made an appointment for a full hysterectomy on November 16; 5 days after my 33rd birthday. Happy Birthday Lisa!

I called a close friend as well as the guy I was seeing at the time, to tell them that I was turning off my phone, going dark, and didn't want to talk to or see anyone until I was finished processing what was going on.

While I knew that I wanted a hysterectomy, to be done with everything, it was still a huge shock. Since I decided so quickly, I didn't have any idea of what to expect after surgery. It was a roller-coaster from hell. I was sent straight into menopause. I now had 2 hormones I would be taking for who knows how long and a whole list of issues that a 33-year-old was not ready for.

At the end of the day, sure, I'm technically a two-time cancer survivor. But in reality, I don't think of myself that way, as a survivor. I just decided that I wasn't giving up. I did the work that needed to be done. I decided not to sit there and wait for someone else to come and save me. I chose to keep going. I decided that I was going to fight. Sure, I had something wrong with me, and I took care of it. I know that each and every one of us has been put on this earth for a reason, to do something. And hell, if I can thrive and persevere through the trials I've experienced, I sure as hell know you can too!

JOB SCREAMED OUT IN PAIN, LIKE HE WAS BEING PRICKED WITH A MILLION DULL NEEDLES, BECAUSE HE BASICALLY WAS. "GOD, THIS REALLY REALLY REALLY SUCKS! WHY DIDN'T YOU JUST KILL ME BEFORE I WAS BORN? I'D RATHER NOT HAVE LIVED AT ALL IF THIS IS WHAT MY LIFE IS GOING TO BE. SERIOUSLY, EVERY PART OF MY MIND, BODY, AND SPIRIT ARE SUFFERING RIGHT NOW AND I'M PRETTY SURE THE LIGHT I SEE AT THE END OF THE TUNNEL, IS A TRAIN."

Job 3:11-26   LOLV

Lisa Marie Heath

You've Gotta Have Faith

I was able to attend school again, graduating with my associate degree, and applied to further my education in psychology because without a higher education in the field there were only a handful of jobs that I'd be able to apply for. I knew that I wanted to do research, have my own practice, and present lectures. Here in Florida, if you attend a local junior college, you have a better chance of being accepted into one of the state universities. My first 3 years are something we'll talk about a little later, for now though, settle in for another thrilling snippet straight from the Life of Lisa. Afterall, we've got a very important date, and don't want to be late!

I decided to apply to three universities but really had my heart set on one. The school at the top of my list accepted me *yay*, but with a pretty big stipulation. I needed to get an A in my last math class, trigonometry. Honestly, when will I ever need to use trigonometry for my work in psychology? I'd already passed statistics with flying colors, shouldn't that have been enough? I did my best, studying as much as humanly possible and my final grade was an 89. My professor at the time knew that I needed to take home an A, and I was definitely pissed off when I saw that I'd finished only 1 point shy. So long school #1. I received an acceptance letter from my #3 school, and while it was exciting to hear that a university was honored to have me, deep down I was totally depressed. I really only applied to that third school as a safety. It wasn't somewhere I saw myself actually attending. Now, while I'm reflecting on all of this to write the book you're currently reading, I realize that it was a big deal to be accepted into that #3 safety school. I mean, damn Lisa, it was still a mother-flocking university for Pete's sake! About 2 weeks later, I got home and was a little disappointed when I checked the mail only to find the box was empty. When I walked in the door Mom yelled, *"Lisa, you got a package."* I raced through the living room, down the hall, and into my bedroom. There on my desk was a big envelope, a really big one, with the logo I'd been hoping for! It was an acceptance letter from my #2 school. I'd been accepted into not 1 but 2 great universities - take that trigonometry!

    I chose to attend the University of Central Florida (Go Knights!), and during my 3-year stint at UCF, I accomplished a ton of once in a lifetime things. I was cancer free and finally able to be a normal college student. I was driving 3 hours, twice a week to attend classes, was a teacher's aide, and worked on 2 big research projects, one of which was my own. Those years were the absolute best times of my life. While at UCF I was asked by 2 major psychology associations to be a part of an undergraduate thesis symposium on the topic of identity and psychology. Talk about a big deal. It was an absolute honor to be presenting my own research at the Southeastern Psychologist Association in Atlanta, GA. Followed by the 20th Annual Conference of the Society for Research on Identity

Formation, in St. Paul, MN. I've always been passionate about researching individual identities when it comes to nature vs. nurture. Getting to travel to educate others in my field about my research, was amazing and truly lifechanging. I chose to write my honor's thesis on the same topic, which in my opinion today is still a powerful read. Attending and presenting at those conferences were some of my best experiences. Getting to meet so many other like-minded people to discuss the fascinating world of psychology definitely excited my inner psych-nerd.

    While still attending UCF. I took the GRE (General Record Examinations), a standardized test similar to the SAT or ACT, and I bombed. Like, really bad. I don't remember my exact score but trust me when I say that it made me look like an uneducated dropout. I've always worked best at drafting papers, presenting in front of a class, or verbally providing details about a topic, but test taking has never been a strength of mine. Many universities use those GRE results to determine the best students for their school, despite my horrible score, I tried not to let the results get to me and proceeded to apply to 30 different colleges because I knew when I put my mind to something, it was going to happen. Oh, and because I was so great at statistics, I remembered that for every 10 people you ask, on average 1 will say yes, 2 will say maybe, and the rest will be big fat nos. So, by applying to 30 schools, I was set up to have at least 3 accept me, right? Let me tell you, my advisors were not impressed with having to complete 30 different recommendation letters to go with each of those applications, even though they could have used the same one each time. But I digress, again. While waiting for the acceptance letters to start rolling in, I graduated with Honors from UCF with my Bachelor of Science in Psychology, with a minor in Cognitive Sciences.

Over the course of 6 months, it felt like our mailbox was always full. Of course, many of those letters simply said, 'thank but no thanks - all the best with your future endeavors.' Anyone who's ever applied for a higher education knows the drill. Luckily though, after sending my 30 applications into the wind, I received 3 acceptance offers back. I was accepted into Florida State University in Tallahassee, University of South Florida in Tampa, and Flocking Goal Chasing University in Fork Mayers. I accepted a spot at Flocking Goal Chasing University for the simple fact that it was close enough to home that I could visit my parents on the weekends, and their admissions department didn't require that I drive down for an in-person interview. The best part of all was that my GRE score wasn't a factor in their decision. Score!

That summer Mom and I went down to Fork Mayers to find my first apartment away from home. Yes, as a 26-year-old I'd never fully moved out of my parent's house. It's funny, because as I write this, I'm once again sitting in the bedroom I've used since high school, but that's another story, for another day. I knew that Fork Mayers was where the snowbirds like to go but we still couldn't get over how expensive rent was for even the tiniest of studio apartments. Mom and I were at our whit's ends after a full day of what felt like wasted gas, driving around the area using an actual paper map, and finding nothing. By the second day I was on the phone, crying to my dad that I just wanted to come home. I told him it could be just like undergrad school; I'd live at home with them and commute twice a week for class. I love driving, and sure it would make for some really long days with hours spent on the road to and from school, but even paying for all that gas would be less expensive than renting a place in Fork Mayers. Dad told us to hang on and keep looking, at least for one more day. The next morning, I was desperate and started reaching out to Facebook friends, looking in newspapers, and calling realtors to see if they had any ideas of places coming up for rent. Believe it or not I connected with a woman who told me she knew of a place, but that it wasn't going to be available for 2 months, so it wasn't technically listed anywhere yet. I told her that 2 months was perfect, because my classes didn't start until August.

Once again, God had my back, and everything fell into place at just the right time. That afternoon I signed the rental agreement, paid the application fee, and we were back on the road, on our way home to Jacksonville. August 1 finally arrived, and I was able to collect my new keys, deep clean the place, and move into my new gorgeous 2 bedroom, 2 bath, first floor condo, with a pool, and canal access. My commute to school was only 45 minutes which if you're familiar with Florida, you know is nothing at all. Even though I was living further away from campus than most of the other students, I had much better views than my peers, and I was paying tons less than they were. Mom stayed with me that first week while we set everything up and I got things sorted out with my classes. Because I only had in-person courses on Tuesdays and Thursdays, I had a nice long weekend to drive mom back to Jacksonville, pick up my cat, and go back 'home.' The transition from my childhood home to my fancy new condo wasn't too bad once I got used to the noise. There was only one small downside to my new home, it was located right next to a parkway which meant using earplugs for the first few weeks until my subconscious was able to tune out the constant traffic.

Grad school started out surprisingly well. My classes were great although I joked that from day 1, I was already behind the rest of my cohort. Everything was fast paced and more work than my previous research project and thesis had been. I was used to having all the time in the world to get things completed, but that wasn't the case at FGCU. I had only 3 years to get everything done. Game on. That first semester I was focused on making a good impression and showing 'them' that they'd made a great decision, choosing me to be a part of their student body. I went home from time to time, where Dad would ask how things were going. My response was always the same, *"It's going. I'm not really sure how my teachers feel about me though."* Without fail he'd try pushing for more details, but I kept things to myself. I was an adult and any issues I was experiencing were mine to fix. At least that's what I thought at the time.

One of my professors, started showing some pretty blatant favoritism early on in the semester. Luckily, I met and bonded quickly with a girl in my cohort who was, like myself, not a perfect fit for their 'normal mold.' Misfits unite! Between the two of us, we noticed a discrepancy in the attention and support we were receiving in class compared to other students who better fit that mold. Neither of us were selected to answer questions in class and our assignments were being marked up for falling short of the professor's expectations, no matter how many times we wrote and rewrote them based on previous feedback. I live for understanding assignments. Things aren't always worded in the clearest way, but I'm a perfectionist who mastered the art of reading between the lines, so I couldn't understand how I was continuing to miss the mark. By the end of that first semester, I had decent grades, all B's. But, if I got anything lower, I'd be on immediate probation. Understandable of course, but seriously, grad school is no joke.

This specific professor, who for the purpose of this story I'm going to call, The Red Queen, (yes, like Alice in Wonderland) pulled me aside one day after class and let me know that she'd noticed something with my writing. She wanted to know if I'd ever heard about the writing center on campus. I told her that yes, I was familiar with what a writing center is, and that I'd used the writing center at UCF quite a bit while I was drafting my thesis before graduation. The Red Queen, seeming to not hear me, or not care, informed me that the following semester I should make a point of taking any written assignments to the writing center to have someone read over my work. I was shocked and more than a little pissed off. Didn't she realize that I was the only member of the entire cohort who had researched and written a thesis before coming to grad school? Flock! Luckily, this interaction was the last time I would see her before going home for the Holidays.

While on Christmas break, Dad once again asked how things were going. But this time he added, *"Are you planning on going back down to Fork Mayers? I can see the struggle on your face and it's obvious that you're mentally exhausted."* I let him know that he was 100% right about the burnout I was experiencing, and before I could stop myself, I was telling him exactly what was happening.

"My professors think I'm a dumb redneck from Orange Park that doesn't know how to write. In their opinion I ask too many questions and still don't fully understand what they're talking about. They consistently give me the short end of the stick and are very obviously forcing out anyone that doesn't fit or conform to their perfect mold. And guess what, I'm on that list. My first friend within the cohort already let me know that she was leaving the program because she'd had enough. So, tell me Dad, what the hell am I supposed to do?"

"Well Lisa, first, take a few deep breaths. What do you think you should do?"

"I guess if I plan on working with serious cases in my future practice, this whole 'situation' could be a great test of my tolerance and patience. If I can survive in a battle with The Red Queen, I'll know that I can handle anything else that life throws my way."

I made the decision to go back to school after the break but warned Dad that he may be receiving a million and one phone calls asking him to talk me off the ledge.

Going into spring semester I was excited and determined. New year, same Lisa. Ready to remind 'them' not to judge a person by their appearance or way of speaking. Y'all I'm a country girl and unless I'm speaking to a large crowd or presenting in a professional situation, words fly outta my mouth and through the air like sparkles. But no matter how I pronounce things, I'm a damned smart cookie, and I needed them to recognize that. Now, for the sake of not turning this book from an enjoyable read to a massive tome, I'm going to spare you all the fluff and sum up the rest of my FGCU experience pretty quickly. Ready? Let's go.

Spring Semester:

- My schedule included 3 classes and 4 professors
    - Class 1-Counseling Theories & Techniques
        - This is what they refer to as a Crucial Class – one that was required.
        - I was one very happy girl. My binder was three times the sizes of everyone else's. Why might you ask? Well, my binder was going to be my bible after graduation, when I became a counselor with my own practice. By keeping my notes about the techniques, we learned, I knew I would be that much more prepared for my future clients.
    - Class 2-Cross Cultural
        - This class was a nightmare. I will give the professor a little grace because she was new, however her tests were impossible, to the point where we would have to work with each other

to even figure out what her questions were actually asking. Our big assignment, writing a summary and reflection of 2 journal articles or non-fiction publications to be presented to the class, was a team effort, and I was paired with a guy who was already being 'forced out' of the program. This class sealed his fate, and almost mine.

- I nearly failed because of the topic we were assigned, and the way my partner chose to present things. I actually had to plead my case to the professor and luckily, she allowed me to make necessary revisions to better align our project with her outlined expectations and resubmit for a new grade (I got an A in case you were wondering). She also shared with me the feedback she received from 3 of my fellow classmates, *"I felt so bad for Lisa in the presentation, she was so nervous and seemed scared." "So nervous she was having a hard time pronouncing words." "Lisa was nervous, and I empathized with her."*

o Class 3-Practicum

- The focus of this course was to prepare us to be counselors. The first of two steps before our internships started.
- The first half of the semester we were required to attend a conference in psychology and write a paper about it. I was able to attend a

conference being held at my alma mater (UCF), which meant spending a weekend away from Fork Mayers, in a town I knew well. It was a great experience and extremely informative.

- I had no issues with understanding what this professor was asking of us and delivering on those assignments. I was also able to (finally) get over how uncomfortable it was to hear my own voice and critiques played back.

During Practicum we were each given the opportunity to submit our top 3 choices for internships in the fall. This is when I knew for sure that I had a target on my back. I selected my top 3 and submitted them to the professor in charge of the internship program, a woman who I'll call Dodo (as in Dodo Bird ala Alice in Wonderland - there's a theme here) for the sake of this story. It's funny when you think about it, how Dodo birds are now extinct, because as the ecosystem changed these flightless clumsy birds couldn't figure out how to survive. But I digress. One by one Dodo called us to the front of the room to share our assigned internship locations, but, when it was my turn, she informed me that the selections I'd made were only available to 2nd year interns. Of course, this wasn't marked anywhere on the paperwork she'd provided. I was told that I'd need to make a new choice, and because everyone else had already been given their assignments I was left to pick through the few options left over. I took the list of what was still available back to my seat, praying that there might still be a private practice spot open because that was going to be the best way for me to learn how to run my own business in the future. Luckily there was a private Christian counseling center on the list, and I told Dodo I'd take it. I took the necessary paperwork to secure my placement and by the following week I was the only member of the cohort that knew for sure they'd been placed. Take that Dodo.

One evening after a particularly trying day in class, I was on the phone with Dad, going on and on about something that had bothered me more than usual, when he interrupted me to say, *"You need to read Job."* Excuse me? You mean the book in the Bible? Who are you and what have you done with my father? The man who's only ever walked into a church when he absolutely has to, for a funeral or wedding, is telling me that I need to read the Bible?

"Just read it Lisa, trust me."

So, I did. I pulled out my 1984 King James Version of the Bible, given to me by my grandmother Ruby for my first Christmas, and read Job. Now, I'm not going to lie and tell you it was easy, or that it made complete sense right away. Nope. It took me a few days but by the end of the week I had a pretty solid grasp of the underlying message, and why Dad had chosen that book, that story, for me to read. I needed to learn patience and have faith.

Summer Semester:

- 1 class and 1 professor
    - Advanced Practicum
        - We were instructed to focus on using only one of the techniques we'd been taught, on our

'practice clients.' Residents of a senior citizen community, most of them living within the dementia ward, or suffering from Alzheimer's.

The purpose of this course was for us to better understand the difficulties associated with providing counseling to individuals who have gaps in their memories. It absolutely broke my heart talking to these people for hours, asking them to relive parts of their life that they struggled with remembering, knowing that the moment I left, they would have no idea what had happened. I was paired up with a lovely gentleman who I discovered after our first few interactions, loved playing cards. So, instead of sitting awkwardly across from each other, asking him question after question, interview style, we played cards, and he told me about his life. We had conversations instead of interrogations. I learned that he'd lived in Australia at one point in his life, and he got giddy with excitement when he was able to share his stories of adventure. When it came time for me to present what I'd learned from my 'patient interactions' to the class, I explained how we'd been able to connect. I shared that by playing cards he was able to focus on something he enjoyed doing, which seemed to allow his memories to refocus with less confusion. When I presented my findings, I did so by speaking about this gentleman as an individual, a person, not a case study, which as you may have guessed did NOT fly. I was informed that I should only refer to my patients or clients as such, without emotion or connection, only findings and diagnosis.

Fall Semester:

- My schedule included 3 classes and 4 professors
  - Class 1-Mental Disorders
    - This is what they refer to as a Crucial Class – one that was required.
    - During this course we learned how to diagnose and use the DSM5 (*The Diagnostic and Statistical Manual of Mental Disorders, Fifth Edition*). My professor was new to our school and had transferred from a university that held 12-hour classes on the weekends. Let's call her Dr. Jabberwocky, shall we? Dr. Jabberwocky was very matter of fact and no-nonsense. After seeing the syllabus and tentative coursework schedule she'd prepared my excitement for this course popped like a balloon into a million pieces. Looking back at these pages today still overwhelms me.
    - The DSM5 is no joking matter. Clocking in at 1,000+ pages of codes and diagnosis that are integral in the clinical world, this single book is basically the Bible for professionals in the mental health field.

Dr. Jabberwocky handed out case studies to each of us and instructed that we read through them to provide all pertinent diagnoses, supporting information, and treatment plans for the clients in question. During my entire time at FGCU the professors were extremely vocal about working together with the other members of our cohort to work through questions, crowdsource ideas, and support each other through our 3-year journey. They went so far as to suggest that we develop these bonds to ensure that in the future, when we have our own practices, we already have a community of colleagues to lean on when needed.

I'd connected really well with one other member of the cohort, and we'd partnered together on quite a few projects to better understand what we were learning, (2 minds really are better than one) and this assignment was no different. After I turned in my paper, I let my professor and cohort know that I was headed back to Jacksonville for the rest of the week to help around the house while Dad preparing for knee surgery. While I was home, I received an email from Dr. Jabberwocky, to me, with the entire rest of the FGCU faculty cc'd. The email stated that Dr. Jabberwocky and the University Head needed to speak with me as soon as possible about a serious issue. Flock - what now?! I responded that I was at home helping my family, like I'd told them a few days prior, and I wouldn't be returning to campus until the following Tuesday, when we had class next, but that I'd be happy to come in early that day to meet with them.

I was informed that Tuesday was *far* too late. We needed to meet now. So, Skype it was. While I was waiting for them to send over a link for the call I talked to my study-buddy, and she told me that she'd been called for a meeting as well. We figured that this 'issue' had to be something with the papers we'd submitted, but still had no clue what was going on. We'd followed the assignment to the letter and turned in what we thought were accurate diagnoses, treatment plans, and supporting information.

When I logged on for our Skype call, Dr. Jabberwocky was full of leading questions, all with an edge of insinuating that I had cheated or something. I had nothing to hide so I answered their questions truthfully, which they took as my being 'difficult.' The call ended with their telling me they would get back to me with *an official determination on the matter*. A few days later, while still at home in Jacksonville, I got another email from Dr. Jabberwocky. I was being written up for Academic Dishonesty as well as receiving a zero for the assignment. Oh, and by the way, if I didn't withdraw from the course immediately, I would also be receiving an F. So, with no other choice, that's what I did. Dr. Jabberwocky - 1, Lisa - 0.

- Class 2-Clinical Internship 1
  - This is when we finally got to use everything we'd been learning, with actual clients. Seriously, this course was the pinnacle of the entire program. I was super excited to be working with the public and putting what I'd learned into action, that was until I found out that my professor was going to be Dodo, again.

During out first class meeting we were split into small groups, with an assigned group supervisor. As luck would have it, Dodo was in attendance, and she made sure that I was in her group with two other students, both of whom fit the 'desired mold' just like they should. Yep, I said it. But I wasn't going to let anything stop me. I was still hellbent on mastering this 'patience' thing that I'd been reading and re-reading about in Job. No matter how much it felt like the odds were stacked against me. The following week we met with our respective groups and for the most part the class went fine. I found out what dates I'd be presenting on, when site visits were scheduled, and when I'd be expected to deliver recordings for review. The two big dates I needed to remember were both in October, first for my recordings, and second for my presentation. Dodo fell behind on listening to the recordings for our small group, and I found myself calling and emailing her in an attempt to gather any constructive criticism, recommendations, or changes I needed to be making. Now remember at the time, I lived a solid 45 min drive away from campus and was going broke paying for gas to get from my condo to school and back twice a week, as well as going to my onsite counseling sessions for my internship. I communicated to Dodo that I was able to come in early on any Tuesday before class to meet with her, but I didn't have the resources to make the extra drive during the week. She quickly escalated this into my 'refusing to meet with her' and got the FGCU Faculty Head involved to report my insubordination. Seriously, you can't make this shit up.

We finally got things straightened out and set up a meeting for the following Tuesday, 90 minutes before class was set to start, and I was scheduled to give my presentation. I reported to her office at the designated time and Dodo asked that I follow her into a separate meeting room. My heart sank into my gut. I knew right away that something was wrong. When Dodo and I entered the room, my professor from summer semester was already there waiting, and the two of them quickly began detailing how I wasn't a right fit for this program, or for the university. For 30 minutes I was told that it had been noticed since Advanced Practicum that I wasn't picking things up like other students. My recordings weren't consistent, and I was not following the instructions of utilizing a 'solution focused' technique with my clients. They told me in no uncertain terms that I didn't fit the mold and the recommendation was that I start looking at other program options. I sat there utterly defenseless, sobbing, unable to speak or provide a response to the things they were saying. I wanted to tell them, of course my recordings are varied, I have 4 different clients, with 4 different treatment plans, and I AM utilizing the solution focused technique, in fact that's exactly what I was scheduled to present to the class in less than an hour.

    The meeting was over as quickly as it had started and I was left in complete shock, covered in tears, snot, and physically shaking. Before rushing to the nearest bathroom, I asked Dodo if I could reschedule my presentation in light of what had just taken place. She advised me that if I chose not to present today, I would receive a zero for the assignment, so I should go splash some water on my face because I only had a few minutes before class was going to start. I grabbed my phone, ran to the bathroom and called one of my closest friends.

"Hey."

"Hey Lisa. Don't you have class this evening?"

"Yea. It starts in a few minutes."

"How'd the meeting go? I didn't think I'd hear from you until tonight."

"The meeting was… well, let's just say my plans have changed."

"Lisa… what are you going to do?"

"I'm gonna commit educational suicide."

"WHAT DOES THAT EVEN MEAN?! Are you sure you know what you're doing?

"Yep. I don't know what's going to happen tomorrow, but I know what I'm doing right now. Gotta go though, I don't wanna be late."

I splashed some cold water on my face, looked in the mirror, wished myself luck & made the decision that whatever happened, the Red Queen and her army would not win. Not today. As I walked down the hall I focused on my breathing, wiped away any lingering tears, and held my head high. When I walked into the classroom, I took my place at the front of the class and began presenting my case study. I'd been working with a woman, a pastor's wife, who had five children, had recently moved from Nebraska to Florida, and wanted a divorce. During our first meeting, she told me without hesitation that she was done. She was desperate for an escape from her marriage and had no desire to try working things out with her husband. But she came back and met with me for 6 weeks, and when we were finished working together, she was a much happier woman, she was content in her marriage, and confident in her path going forward. Bam! Solution Focused!

Dodo asked how it was that I thought this client had been able to overcome her previous issues and decide that she didn't want to divorce her husband after all. Without hesitation I looked her dead in the face and responded, *"God."* Of course, this was not the answer she'd expected, and wanted to know why I would say that.

"Well, because we prayed together at the end of every session."

Dodo's face turned bright red, and she shouted, *"You can't do that!"* I calmly explained that my internship was with a Christian Counseling Center, and my client was a pastor's wife. Her religion was a very important part of her life, and if praying to God at the end of our sessions brought her peace and clarity, I saw nothing wrong with it. At the end of class Dodo pulled me aside and informed me that what I'd done was inappropriate and she in no way approved of this kind of behavior. I knew that by making the admission during my presentation that I prayed with my client, I was going to be told to withdraw immediately. And, after the morning I'd been through, I was completely okay with it.

Within the week I was asked to meet with the FGCU faculty and when I arrived on campus, I remember feeling like I was walking into my own funeral. Cue the procession music. I even wore all black on purpose. When I arrived, they were all already seated around the room looking at me.

"Let's begin," said the Red Queen.

"What are the charges?"

Dodo read from the scroll. *"She's different, odd, and a little kookie. She thinks outside the box, knowingly defies orders, and blatantly rebelled against your army, your majesty."*

"Off, Off, Off, with her head!" Shouted the Red Queen.

At least that's what I heard. The words they used may have been different, but the message was the same. I'm sure they discussed in detail all of the things they'd brought up in past meetings and came to the conclusion that my best course of action would be to drop my last class, take a break, really think about what I wanted to do, and decide if I was the 'right fit' for FGCU and this program. All of which could have easily been summed up in an email for documentation purposes, and to save me a tank of gas. But, when you bully someone in person, verbally, there's no proof to worry about.

My birthday was coming up as well as the holiday weekend, so I decided that it was the perfect time to move back home to Jacksonville. I still had one class left, with a group presentation coming up in a few weeks, so I let my partners know that I wasn't going to be on campus, but I would be back for our presentation, and was available via email or phone if they needed me to help with anything other than what I'd already been assigned. Even though my time at FGCU was coming to an abrupt end, I didn't want to leave my classmates high and dry. I drove back to school on the day of our presentation, and informed my professor that I was going to take some time off to consider everything they'd said. She told me that she'd let the board know my decision, and that was that.

- Class 3-Does it even matter anymore?!
  - This was the only class that I completed this semester, and I did so with an A! But of course, because of what had transpired with my other 2 classes, it didn't matter anymore. I'd been not-so-gracefully pushed out of the program and urged to withdraw from classes to 'take time off.'

Flocking Goal Chasing University my ass! More like Flocking Goal CRUSHING University. Flockers.

THROUGH UGLY SNOT-BUBBLE-FILLED SOBS JOB BEGGED, "GOD, IF YOU WOULD JUST TELL ME WHAT I DID TO BECOME YOUR TARGET I WOULD ASK YOU TO FORGIVE ME. SERIOUSLY, WHAT COULD I HAVE DONE TO PISS YOU OFF SO BAD? HAVE I OFFENDED YOU? AM I A BURDEN? YOU'VE GOT TO TELL ME QUICK BEFORE I GIVE INTO MY SUFFERING AND RESIGN MYSELF TO DEATH."

Job 7:20-21 LOLV

Lisa Marie Heath

Limbo

It was December 2014 and I was left wondering what in the blue blazes was I going to do now?! From where I was sitting, I was royally screwed. Thank God my father needed knee surgery and had asked me to move home to help take care of him during his recovery. He said that after he'd fully recovered, we'd figure things out. Just be patient Lisa. At this point, I really wished my father had never told me about the book of Job. I had no Grad school lined up for the spring, and realized I might be better off waiting to enroll somewhere for summer or fall. It felt like I'd just racked up $40,000 in student loans for nothing. If I transferred to another program, I would only be able to take something like 16 of my 32 credits with me – Flocking fabulous! It's fair to say that I was ready to give up.

My supervisor from the Christian Counseling Center had given me a going away gift when my assignment with them ended. It was a framed picture with a shear bow on top, colorful beads strung across the middle, a small cross, and printed on the gray textured background was the message:

"Don't worry about anything instead, pray about everything. Tell God your needs and don't forget to thank Him for His answers." (Philippians 4:6)

So, that's what I did.

"God, it's me, Lisa. You can have everything in my life. Everything I have left that is. You've already taken the dreams I've had for years, to do what? Take care of my parents? Which is something I was already doing. I love my parents, but also, let's be real. I was just forced out of a program, won't be able to attend another university until at least next fall, and have zero clue what area of study I'll pursue if I am even able to register somewhere new. My relationship with psychology is over, which kills me to say, because it's been my rock for so long. I don't know God; I just don't know. So, it's all yours. All of it. You won."

A few days later a friend of mine told me that her church was hosting online services. It was obvious that she was trying to subtly push me in that direction, and I started looking into her church, what time their services were held, and how I might be able to watch them online. The next morning when I woke up, I grabbed my computer, clicked on the church's website to continue my research, and my screen filled with a countdown. 5…4…3…2…1. Talk about divine timing. The service music started, and I hurried to mute my microphone, grab a cup of coffee, and settle in. When I got back to my computer, the pastor was speaking, and I contemplated closing out the window and going back to bed. Lord knows I wasn't thrilled about watching or hearing a sermon right now. I was grieving a huge death of identity, feeling completely lost, hopeless, and alone. I was embarrassed that my dream, my passion, and my love for helping others in a client setting was over. Everything I'd dreamt about doing, having my own practice, conducting research, it was all gone. Instead of listening to the pastor I was throwing myself a pity party. Then, something he said caught my attention. To this day I can't tell you what it was that he said. But when I looked at my computer screen, like really looked, and focused on what this man was saying…within moments, I was in tears. His message hit home for me, not necessarily even the words he was saying, but the passion and spirit behind them. I felt a draw, a pull, to reclaim my own relationship with God. Right then and there. The church itself was non-denominational, open-minded, and seemed pretty cool. It was like no church I had ever been to before, and it wasn't long before I was attending their services on a semi regular basis. I found a new set of friends that were amazing, and one Sunday, when the church was having water baptisms, I felt in my gut that I wanted to participate. The problem was that I didn't have any extra clothes, not to mention that it was a frigidly cold January morning. After going back and forth with myself, I said screw it!

I was all in with my newfound faith. It's common, in the church world, to see an influx of individuals wanting to serve their congregation in some way after committing or recommitting to their faith, not a bad thing at all, and I was no different. The following month the congregation was asked to participate in the *Daniel Fast*. Don't know what that is? No worries, I sure as heck didn't until I asked either. I was directed to the Bible and told all about what the *Daniel Fast* entailed.

"For three whole weeks, Daniel gave into his grief and icky human emotions. He refused to eat anything enjoyable. No savory roast beast, cheesy delights, chocolate

desserts. His plates were nearly empty with only a few plain nibbles. For 21 days he didn't shower, bathe, shave, or drink a single sip of wine – which was basically unheard of." (Daniel 10: 2-3 LOLV)

After learning what foods I would be giving up, I nearly died. Bread. Seriously? There was one special kind of bread that was approved of, but it tasted horrible, so I wound up giving up rolls, toast, bagels, all of it, for three whole weeks. I gave it my all to adhere the best I could to the diet. Did I mention that at the same time, I was in the middle of training for a half marathon? It felt like I was trying to kill myself, just to get closer to God and still have a life here on earth. I will say that being *that* fatigue honestly had me feeling more and more okay with letting go of how I saw my life going.

During service on the third to last day of the fast, I heard a voice in my left ear saying, *"You're going to be up there."* Now, I may be crazy, but I'd never heard voices before. I mean, I've heard my thoughts, but this wasn't *my* voice, this was straight up a male's voice in my ear. Spooky. I tried to shake it off and convince myself that I was just hearing things because of the lack of carbs in my life. But, the following day at service I heard the same voice, this time in my right ear, *"You're going to be a speaker."* This time it was a little harder to ignore. I started really questioning my choice to commit so strongly to the *Daniel Fast,* since it was obviously messing with my body and subconscious. On the last day of the fast, while the congregation was quietly praying, I heard the voice again, this time in both ears, and nearly shouting. *"You're going to be a pastor."* I'm pretty sure I responded out loud that time, *"What?!"* Seriously though. I curse like a sailor. How would someone like me ever be called to be a pastor and lead others?

The next morning when I woke up, I still couldn't shake the voices and messages I'd been hearing and asked my dad, *"If someone was telling you to do something kind of crazy, would you do it?"* Of course, he wanted to know what the heck I was talking about, and I filled him in on what I'd been experiencing over the last few days. I told him that God had been telling me I was going to be a speaker, a pastor. Dad, being the man he is, said, *"Well Lisa, if that's what God's telling you to do, you should probably do it."*

Of course, this new direction would require additional schooling, but at least this time I knew what I was meant to be doing, and that God was on my side. I applied to 3 schools, Hillsong in Australia (yes, that Hillsong), Liberty University, and Southeastern University in Lakeland. I decided on attending Southeastern University, because it was within driving distance from home, and started taking courses with a focus on Theology. Yes me, a foul-mouthed gal from Florida studying theology. I didn't understand it either but who was I to question God.

Lisa Marie Heath

JOB LET OUT A DEEP PAINED BREATH AND EXPLAINED TO HIS FRIENDS, "YOU CAN'T SERIOUSLY BE SUGGESTING THAT I ARGUE WITH GOD. HE'S PROFOUND AND POWERFUL. HE CAN MOVE MOUNTAINS, SHAKE THE EARTH, AND TURN THE SUN OFF WITH A SNAP OF HIS FINGERS. DO YOU SEE ME? I'M MORTAL, I'M BROKEN, AND I'M BASICALLY DEAD. HE COULD SQUASH ME RIGHT WHERE I AM WITHOUT EVEN BREAKING A SWEAT."

Job 9:2-20   LOLV

Lisa Marie Heath

Have Faith, Will Travel

I was so happy to have an idea of the direction my life was headed, even if I was walking blindly. I decided to start classes in the fall, taking the summer for myself before jumping back into a master's program. The cool thing about starting my new program in the fall was that I was able to earn school credits for completing an internship at the church I was already attending. Double win. I love when I'm able to learn firsthand while I'm studying and putting things into practice right away. I really loved the youth. In my internship I was able to work hand in hand with middle schoolers and it was truly special. During the first semester of my internship, I realized that because I didn't grow up in church, or spend my own youth volunteering, I was considered an outcast. I wrongly assumed that at my age, people wouldn't make snap judgements or treat me differently, but man was I wrong. I found myself having to explain repeatedly why I was doing what I was doing. I did things my way, I always have, and I learned quickly that was NOT the right decision. One of my supervisors called me into a meeting and verbally scolded me, telling me that I wasn't doing a good job and getting upset that I was sitting in what she considered to be, a defensive state. At the time I was sitting cross-legged on the floor, with my arms resting on my knees, if anything, I considered my position to be extremely open and comfortable. But obviously I was wrong.

At the end of the meeting, she gave me an assignment to go and talk to 5 of my closest friends, asking them to share with me one of my negative traits. She also wanted me to ask them how they saw me, what they thought of me. Walking out of that meeting, I decided that this was going to be my only semester doing an internship. The advisors within the program were pushing me out and at the end of the semester I made the decision to adjust my area of study to pursue a career I felt extremely drawn to. Chaplin in the United States Navy. The idea made perfect sense. I cussed as much as they did, I was real and didn't sugarcoat things. It sounded perfect. I wanted to be sent overseas to serve as the Chaplin who meets our men and women when they arrive at the hospital from the war zone. I was prepared and knew it would be hard, but my heart has always been with the military, so this path seemed like a win-win.

During my second semester, I ended up having to withdraw from at least one class. I struggled with courses focused on the Old Testament and instead of getting an F, I withdrew from those classes. Sometimes getting my tuition back, other times I didn't.

By summer I had no idea how I'd been passing the classes I did. I wrote and submitted what I thought they were looking for, but without having an undergraduate in theology, I was totally lost. While trying desperately to understand the material every assignment took me so much longer than it should have. My mom tried to help by skimming the chapters of the Old Testament while I worked on other assignments, but between us, we both had no clue. It's funny now looking back and realizing that I was only passing those classes by the grace of God. I submitted assignments immediately after I finished writing them, without rereading or double-checking anything. I turned in work that was on topic but so far out of the box that at times I wondered if the instructors were even reading what I'd submitted. I'm sure some of the professors looked at my work shaking their heads and thinking, *"How did she even get into this program?"* By the summer semester my student advisor and I were speaking so frequently that we were basically friends. He was super patient with my trying out so many different programs, praying desperately that *this one* would be the one to fit. As the summer was running smoothly, I got an email from him that said, *"Lisa, I think we finally have a program that would be a great fit for you. When do you have a moment to speak?"* I called him back immediately.

"Tell me more about this perfect program."

"Well, it requires some traveling."

"Really?"

"It doesn't have a solid focus in theology. It's more of a leadership and business degree. You'd be learning how to plant churches and run them."

"Oh, I like the sound of that."

"Plus, you've already completed a lot of the required courses, meaning you'd be able to graduate in the winter of 2017."

And just like that we switched my degree once more, and I began studying to be a Ministerial Leader and Church

Planter. The best part was that I was going to be able to travel to different states, studying with some of the best theologians in the world.

Our first class was in Tampa and at the time I was already working with a team planting a church there. We were going to be spending time near Clearwater, which was the perfect place to start this program. When I walked into that first class, I was one of the first to arrive and I was so nervous that I was shaking. Aside from my internship most of my classes had been online. As more people started to arrive, I recognized a familiar face. It was the man who'd been presenting the sermon when I reclaimed my faith. Now my stomach was in my chest. My 'classmates' turned out to be big hitters already working with well-known churches. I was equally intimidated, excited, and nervous. They knew this stuff inside and out and were already living this life. There were only 2 of us in class that weren't associated with huge churches. I felt like the black sheep of the class. I was the one who was different. I asked all the questions, seriously, all of them, because I desperately wanted to understand everything. When that class was over, I went home crying.

"Why God? I'm not understanding my purpose in these classes and projects."

The assignments we were given made sense to me more than any I'd had before, which was a huge relief. And I decided to stop feeling bad about asking questions. God led me here, to this program, to these classes, and he created me the way he did on purpose. Endless questions and all.

I never stopped asking questions, much to the annoyance of my professors and classmates, but I also walked in faith knowing that this was my path. I finished that semester and was ready for winter break. I knew that I was less than a year away from graduation and it was ex~~cit~~ing to be so close to achieving my goal.

The next place we traveled was Washington DC. This was my favorite class, and I made some amazing memories with my cohort. We travelled as a group all over the city and have so many great pictures. The trip really brought us all closer. My cohort even went on to create a meme of our professor and I after an afternoon where I may have asked one too many questions of our theology professor regarding the lamb or goat that was being carried on shoulders during a pilgrimage. I desperately wanted to know the size of the animal. As well as if it was a child carrying it or an adult. The professor was pissed off because he couldn't give a clear answer and was getting frustrated beyond belief at my persistence. What can I say, I like to have as much information as I can to better understand things. He finally snapped, saying, *"No more talk of the lamb. I don't want to hear it."* Oops. I can't say that I was sorry though. The whole reason I was going to school was to ask questions that my someday congregation may want to know. I didn't want to look like I didn't have the answer. That's the thing about faith. Nothing is concrete. The Bible was written by men then it was translated. I think it's like the game of telephone. Which isn't a bad thing. It just shows that everyone isn't a saint. I am 100% convinced that multiple books are missing from the Bible. I mean, where are all the females? God has always been about both of his children, the men, and women. But I digress. I connected with the members of my cohort so strongly that the bonds we formed kept me going when I still didn't really understand what I was doing.

The next place we travelled to was Philly, where we saw the Pirates play. During this trip I realized that I was focusing on enjoying my last few months of freedom. It may sound bad now, but I knew that I needed to get all the crazy out of my system before I officially entered the world of church planting. I'm not a party girl by any means, but I knew that my phase of going out drinking with friends every night was ending. And I was okay with that chapter coming to a close. Summer in Florida is filled with beaches, boating, friends, drinks, and so much sun. With that being said, I enjoyed the heck out of that summer, and no matter how excited I was for my future, I still didn't want this summer to end.

It happened though, the summer came and went. When my last semester started, I knew for the first time that I was doing what I was meant to. Everything made sense. Until my life was upended completely, again.

GOD IS MY HOMEBOY, MY BACKUP, MY CHEERLEADER, MY TRAINER, MENTOR, AND SAVIOR. I'VE NO REASON TO FEAR EARTHQUAKES, TSUNAMIS, HURRICANES, OR CROWDS OF SQUEALING TEENS, BECAUSE I KNOW HE'S ALWAYS WATCHING OUT.

Psalm 46:1-3   LOLV

Lisa Marie Heath

Crash

When we last left off, I was about to graduate with my master's degree in theology, when out of the blue I got a phone call from the Flamingo Lakes Bar & Grill. For the life of me I can't remember what his name was, so let's just call him Bo. Bo was calling to ask if I'd be interested in interviewing for their open Bar Manager Position. Shocked and a bit confused at how he'd gotten my number, I told him that I was definitely interested, and we made plans to meet up later in the week. When I arrived at the bar, I couldn't help but notice that it was located in the nucleus of town, surrounded by all of the other smaller towns that make up Clay County. The restaurant itself was breathtaking, to say the least. I still can't even begin to imagine how much the owners had invested in the building alone. Trust me when I say that it took a full two weeks for me to notice the craziest of details that had been carved into the trees. Bo & I sat down at one of the booths and ordered a drink and appetizers for me to sample. He explained that the owners had hired him to help turn their business around since it was losing money on the daily. The owners, it turned out, had never owned a restaurant or bar in their lives, so this actually was their first rodeo.

Now I knew right then that this was a bad idea. I should've listened to my gut, gotten back in my car & headed for home. But I didn't. I saw the position as an opportunity to gain more experience both behind the bar and in managing a team. Bo let me know that the restaurant currently had a 'decent' bar manager, and if hired, he'd want me to learn everything I could about running the place directly from him. The next thing I knew, Bo was waiving down one of the owners, Rick, an older man with a cowboy hat and a slow, methodical strut. When he joined us in the booth he smelled distinctly of bourbon, and while it was only 1 or 2 in the afternoon, I guess the saying's true, 'it's 5'o-clock somewhere.' That was the first red flag I let slip by. Rick proceeded to look me up, and down, and back up again - yuck - and I guess he liked what he saw because I got the job. Red flag number two.

The two men asked about my experience as a bartender and manager, and I answered them truthfully. While I had plenty of experience behind the bar, I'd never worked as a bar manager before, but I was eager to learn. Rick told me the position was mine, and that he'd let his wife know - we'll come back to her later. I was introduced to Jason, the current bar manager, and it was obvious right away that Rick had forgotten to tell him that he was hiring someone else. Red flag number three, for those keeping count. Before I left, Jason told me that he'd do his best to work me into the schedule and asked for my number and availability. Right away, he texted me his number and I made my way toward the exit. As soon as the door closed behind me, I took one of those deep, loud breaths, the ones I usually only took when I was completing half marathons.

While walking to my car I started talking to God. Although, if anyone was listening, I'm sure it sounded more like I was talking to myself than the Lord. But ask me, did I care? Nope.

"Hey God, it's me, Lisa. So umm... what have I gotten myself into here?"

"I mean, I'm not even sure that I've officially accepted the position, I gave the guy my number though, so I guess I did?"

"I need the job. And this should pay alright, plus the tips, which are my favorite part of bartending. Having cash on hand is always nice."

"My last semester of my master's degree starts in August, and if I'm smart, I can bank the money to use then. I'll be traveling to Atlanta once more in October, but if this position works out the way I hope, everything should fall into place nicely."

A note for you, my dear reader. When your gut tells you to walk away, do it. It's God, The Universe, your higher self, or whatever you believe in telling you that whatever it is you're contemplating, is NOT a good idea. Trust me and learn from my mistakes.

By that weekend Jason had messaged me with a schedule for the following week. I texted back that I was looking forward to working with everyone and had forgotten to ask about the dress code. I sent along a picture of a pair of shorts and asked him if they would be okay. Thankfully he said they'd be great, which was a small win for me. Not having to buy a new wardrobe for a new job. Thank the Lord!

My first few shifts went well. Jason was a good teacher behind the bar, and he figured out really quickly that I'd never worked in a traditional restaurant bar. There were a few bumps while I was training, as there always are. One of the other female bartenders told me during a shift that I was wearing the wrong color of shorts. I let her know that Jason had told me they were fine, along with all the other shorts I'd been wearing to work, so, if she had an issue with them, she should probably take it up with him. Remember how I told you that one of the owners, Rick, had given the greenlight on hiring me? Well, when his wife got back from her vacation she came into the bar one day, sat her stuff down on a chair, and walked off. Without a single word of acknowledgment to me. She came back to the bar wanting to know where Jason was. When I let her know that he was outside at the other bar, she and her resting bitch face stomped off to find him. Turned out that Creepy Rick had forgotten to tell his wife, Tess, that he'd hired me, a female bartender. She proceeded to throw a fit about being kept out of the loop and told Jason that he needed to fire me right away. Luckily, Jason told her that he hadn't hired me, so he wasn't going to fire me. Ha! You may be wondering; how do I know so much about their conversation? Well, I may or may not have been watching and listening from the other side of the door. Tess stormed out of the bar, jumped in her truck, and we didn't see her again for the rest of the day.

I'm a quick learner so I picked things up pretty quickly, especially since Jason was willing to give me extra practice for mixing the bar's specialty drinks at his house. By the third week, I was able to handle the bar by myself, even though I still felt like their menu had way too many food and drink options. But what do I know? Jason and I started hooking up after the 4th of July. This was the summer before I was going to graduate with my master's degree in theology and officially join the 'church world.' I fully embraced having a summer of fun. Drinking more than I usually did, and hanging with people that were wild and crazy, much more so than the folks I was used to spending time with. This new crowd of friends loved to drink and be on the water, it really was what most people think of as the perfect Florida summer. To be honest, I never really fit in with that group, they were Jason's friends, but he always invited me along and I love the water, so I'd suck it up and join the party.

That summer was when everything flipped. One day I'd arranged to swap shifts with Jason so I could get off early since I was opening up the next morning. I was in the car, on my way to work, jamming out in my Celica to 'Fix a Drink' by Chris Janson. I remember thinking it was a very appropriate song choice, since I was on my way to the bar to fix drinks. LOL. While I was sitting at a red light my phone rang and it was Tess, Creepy Rick's wife. She let me know that my services were no longer needed, and when I asked why, she told me that she'd gotten several complaints from patrons of the restaurant as well as other waitresses that they had issues working with me. She told me that my check and tips would be at the bar the following Tuesday (payday) and that was it. I ended the call with a quick thank you, have a good day, and since I now found myself with a clear schedule, I headed for Jason's house.

When I got there and told him what had happened, as well as that since we'd swapped shifts, and I'd been canned, he was now late for work, he was shocked. Turns out he was in the dark too. The next day Jason messaged me to meet him for lunch, and while we were eating, he told me that Tess had fired me because I was pregnant with his (Jason's) child, and she'd been getting complaints from the other female bartender about it. *spoiler: I wasn't pregnant with his or anyone else's child. * He went on to tell me that he was pretty sure she'd coached the waitresses on what to say to build their case against me. While I enjoyed the paycheck and tips, and a few of the other employees, there was no love lost in my being finished at the Flamingo Lakes Bar & Grill.

Jason and I continued hanging out and hooking up, but he'd made it clear that he wasn't looking for a relationship. I was fine either way, as long as he wasn't hooking up with anyone else. Yuck. That football season his mother came to visit and when she did, she took a picture of the two of us, announcing to all of Facebook, 'Look at this cute couple.' By October we were officially in a committed relationship. My last semester of school was fully underway, and I was preparing to travel to Atlanta for the last in-person class of my degree. I was super excited because Jason was going to join me on the trip, and because he was more familiar with Atlanta than I was, he was going to plan things for us to do when I got out of class. October 15th, I was preparing to leave the next day to head up to Georgia, when Jason called to let me know that he had to work and couldn't come with me to Atlanta as planned. *If you remember, he was a bartender, which is probably the easiest kind of shift to get covered.* I made the drive to Atlanta alone, which I honestly didn't mind. I love driving alone, but the fact that Jason had bailed on our plans at the last minute, pissed me off. For the sake of time, I'm going to skip a few details here, but don't worry they'll all be in a follow-up book.

Jason did a lot of stupid stuff. He broke up with me for no reason at all, and while in hindsight I should have cut my losses, I didn't. Because I'd already bought some sexy AF Michael Kors heels without him in Atlanta, for a wedding we were attending together, and there was no way I was letting them go to waste. The next day during class, my professor could tell that something was wrong. He suggested that I head home. He knew firsthand from his own experience traveling, how chaos can happen at home. The next morning, Jason and I spoke in person. Since the wedding was in two days, he asked if I would still go with him. Duh, I had my shoes that he knew nothing about.

Now, if you need to stop and take a break of any kind (bathroom, snacks, drink, let the dog out) I'd recommend doing it now. You really don't want to miss this next part.

These next few pages have been the hardest for me to write. I've started and stopped at least a dozen times and finally had to record my experience verbally to come back and put it onto the page. Revisiting these memories never fails to bring me to tears and threatens to break me like nothing else ever has. But this is a part of my story. And that's what you're here to read.

It was October of 2017 when I opened my eyes and all I could see was the ceiling. I closed my eyes and all I could feel was the pounding and throbbing of my head. It sounded like someone was inside my skull with a jackhammer. As I opened my eyes again, I knew that everything was wrong. I wiggled my toes and was relieved to find that I could move them, but I still didn't know what was going on. I don't know if I fell asleep or passed out from the pain, but the next time I opened my eyes, I looked up to the ceiling and cried to God.

"I don't know what happened."

"I'm scared."

"All I can do is lay here and give you everything because I don't know what's going on."

"I am really scared."

"Please protect me and help me through this."

Sometime later, who knows how short or long, I woke up again and could see out of the corner of my eye, my dad sitting against the wall of my room. My eyes were swollen, foggy, and barely able to open but I knew that the figure beside my bed was my dad.

This entire day was a blur. I know I woke up again and my friend Brittany was beside my bed. She'd just finished running a 5k, a race that I was meant to have been at, cheering her on from the finish line. She came to the hospital as soon as she'd heard what happened to me. Of course, I still didn't know what had happened to me, but if they'd told me, I don't know that I'd have remembered anyway. Brittany asked if I wanted to see what I looked like. She offered to take a picture with her phone, but I told her that I really didn't want to see myself. She took them anyway, and I'm honestly glad she did. I was feeling lost, confused, afraid, and in so much pain, that I knew if I were to see what I looked like in this moment, I may not have the will to survive.

When my mom and dad got back to my room, I realized that I didn't know where any of my stuff was. My purse, my wallet, my glasses, my phone. It's funny what becomes a priority when you're experiencing trauma. Our brains try to grasp for anything that might be 'normal,' and for me, that was my phone. I had an intense need to contact my friends, to let them know where I was, and see if they might be able to tell me anything about what had happened since my memory was a complete blank. My parents told me they didn't know where my phone was. That no one had been able to find it yet, and the assumption was that it was still at the scene.

"What scene?" I asked.

"The scene of the crash." Mom said.

Sometime later, Jason got to the hospital with my phone. He told me that they'd found it at the base of a tree and after he'd had a chance to go home, shower, and get some sleep, he wanted to bring it back to me. He asked how I was feeling. Word of advice to anyone reading this, if you're visiting a friend in the hospital after they've been in a horrible crash, where they're unable to move, are covered with gashes, bruises, blood, and stitches, don't ask how they're feeling. Just, don't.

"How am I feeling Jason? I feel like I got hit by a mother flocking Mac truck. I can't hear myself when I talk, all I can

hear is a constant ear-piercing buzzing sound. I'm stuck in a neck brace and can't move. I hurt, everywhere. I can't cough. I can barely breathe without wanting to cry. My head feels like it's going to explode. I lay here in torture."

The next time I woke up, I was being taken for an MRI and CT scan. I could hear my parents and Jason talking between themselves inside my room.

It took 3 nurses to lift me up and into the MRI machine because I couldn't move at all on my own. As soon as they settled me onto the table and moved me into the MRI tube I was overwhelmed by the sounds of the machine. It sounded as if a jet airplane was hovering over my head. I pushed the emergency button almost immediately, and when they pulled me out of the machine, I told them I couldn't do it. It hurt too much. It was decided that they would give me additional pain meds and run the CT scan while they waited for the drugs to take effect, to hopefully retry the MRI in a bit. But it was still too painful, and the nurses made the call that we would try to get an MRI at a later time. As they were wheeling me down the hall, I begged the nurse beside me to make them leave. I told her between tears that I just needed to be alone. To have quiet. To sleep. When I got back to my room the nurse had done as I'd asked, and my room was blissfully quiet.

Every time I woke up, I asked what had happened to me, what was going on, what was wrong. But everyone, my parents, my friends, the nurses, all told me that we should wait until the doctor was there to answer my questions. I was so scared, confused, and alone.

The next time I opened my eyes, my CrossFit coach was standing beside my bed, with his 3-year-old daughter and a beautiful bouquet of flowers in his arms. It meant so much to me, that he was there to check on me, but before we could really talk, a nurse was rushing them out of the room. Children weren't allowed in the ICU, and flowers were a huge no-no as well. Something about contamination. *(Rolling my eyes.)* She offered to take the vase and flowers and place them at the nurse's station outside my room, so I could see them through the window. Of course, being stabilized in a neck brace and being unable to move meant that I couldn't see anything other than the ceiling and the wall in front of me, but she didn't seem concerned about that.

Thanks to copious amounts of drugs, I was able to sleep through the night, and when I woke up the next morning the doctor was beside my bed. While much of this time was a fog, I'll never forget the first words that the doctor said to me.

"Well, you know you're fucked, right?"

"Excuse me?"

"Yea, you did a really good number on yourself. You've broken and fractured 13 bones, your ear was nearly ripped off and had to be stitched back onto your head, you have a brain bleed that we're keeping under constant surveillance, you have a concussion, have broken your c4-c6 vertebrae, 3 ribs, and 3 bones in your face."

Later in the day, an Orthopedic specialist came to see me, making me sit up and try to move, I started bawling uncontrollably, which only made the pain worse. I was fitted for a brace that wrapped around my torso, holding me in place from my neck down past my stomach. I wasn't able to move my head, my neck, or my core, and I was told that I needed to wear it for at least 3 months. There are no words to describe that feeling. The pain, the weakness, the devastation, the overwhelm. At that moment I was told that I wasn't going to be able to sit up on my own, brush my own hair or teeth. I was going to be completely dependent on others for my basic needs. As a headstrong independent woman, this realization absolutely killed me.

Sitting in my room at the hospital, sobbing from the pain, both physical and emotional, I prayed to God again.

"Please help me get through this. I want to give up. It hurts to breathe. It hurts to cry. My body is broken. Yes, the doctor told me what happened to my body, but it still doesn't make sense. Nothing makes sense. How did I get here, God? I need you to help me. I need you to take care of me. Because I can't do it myself."

This was my life for 2 days in the ICU and another day in a regular room. Nurses, doctors, and visitors filtered in and out of my room at all hours of the day and night, while I lay in bed, unable to move and constantly crying from the physical pain, and fear of how I was going to make it through this experience. It was on the 3rd day that I realized I wasn't going to be able to go home with my mom and dad when I was discharged. There was simply no way that they were going to be able to help with lifting me out of bed, to the bathroom, the shower, etc. No matter how much they wanted to, they were both getting older and weren't physically able to help without hurting both of us. This brought with it the knowledge that I wasn't going to be able to see my puppy who truly was a huge emotional support for me, being that she was so young she constantly jumped up and wanted to play. My only option was to stay with Jason, who at the time was living with his best friend Chad. It wasn't until I'd been released from the hospital and was living in a recliner chair at their place, that I would learn who was driving during the crash. Chad. We'll come back to that a little later.

The first night after being discharged from the hospital, Jason slept on an air mattress beside me in the living room, because I was so scared of being left alone. He became my nurse, my nanny, and my caregiver. He was the person who helped me to take my first shower, cleaning the gravel and debris out of my hair while not bothering the stitches that were holding my ear to my head. Do you have any idea how humiliating it is to have to depend on another person for everything in life? I was completely broken, embarrassed, and defeated. There were moments when I prayed that God would take it all away.

After 3 nights, Jason had to go back to work and a real bed, which meant I'd be spending a few hours at my parent's house, so I wasn't completely alone. I still needed help with getting up, going to the bathroom, and so much more. And I was still in crippling pain. Jason drove me to Mom and Dad's place, got me settled into a borrowed recliner chair, and left for his shift. The plan was that when he got off work, in the wee hours of the morning, he would come back to pick me up and take me back to his place. My friend Jessie stopped by to check on me, and as she was leaving, she let Mom know that I was going to need help getting to the bathroom. Mom shouted from the other room, after the front door shut, "Can it wait until Wheel of Fortune is over?" 15 minutes later, I was sobbing in pain as I made my way to the bathroom by myself. I don't fault my parents for anything, I genuinely believe they didn't understand the severity of the situation. When Jason got off work, he came back to the house to pick me up, and from that point forward, I stayed at his place, whether he was home or at work.

The next night I was in so much pain that Jason offered me a drink. I definitely don't condone mixing prescription medication and alcohol, but at the time, it was the only way I could numb the pain and calm my thoughts. This continued for the next few weeks, during which time I contacted my professor and let them know what had happened. He assured me that I shouldn't worry about anything. The majority of my assignments were already completed, and the few that weren't, could be overlooked due to the situation. He wanted my focus to be on healing myself physically, emotionally, and mentally. The one assignment I held firm that I wanted to complete was a 10-minute sermon that I'd already written and could record for him to review. I held it together while recording my sermon, cracking jokes about being in a neck brace, and how they should 'see the other guy.' But as soon as I was finished, I broke down again, screaming at God asking if I could just be done on this earth?

As I recovered over the next few weeks, I noticed that I would lose periods of time, sometimes only a few moments, other times, hours. There were also times when I could tell I was acting in a way that wasn't like myself. I was depressed, mean, and hateful. I was hurting and the people around me were the same people who had hurt me. I didn't understand any of what was happening. One moment I would be fine, feeling like myself, and the next I was laughing maniacally, or crying uncontrollably. I felt like I was completely out of control of myself, my mind, my life, my actions.

In November, I went to see a neurologist, to follow up on the status of my concussion, and ask questions about what I should and shouldn't be doing while I continued to recover. The doctor assured me that I was cleared to do any activities I wanted to, so long as I didn't hit my head. Jason and I both asked multiple times if I was safe to ride four-wheelers and go on boats. The neurologist answered every question with, *"As long as you don't hit your head."* That was it. I continued using alcohol, marijuana, and pain medication to numb the pain and distract myself from my current situation. With the neurologist's blessing, I spent days out on the speedboat with friends, four-wheeling off-road, and acting like everything was fine. Sure, everything still hurt, like a lot, but I'd been told that I was going to be okay, so I lived like it was.

At the end of the month, over the Thanksgiving holiday, I learned that my cousin had been murdered. News that once again threatened to break me to my very core. But there was no time for me to process this unbelievable loss in my life because it was time to graduate in a couple of weeks. I remember thinking that there was no way my life could get any worse. I'd been physically, mentally, and emotionally broken. I'd lost my cousin, one of my absolute favorite people in the world. But I had no idea what the next year was going to bring.

Lisa Marie Heath

JOB LOOKED TO THE SKY AND HUMBLY SAID, "GOD, I OWE YOU MY LIFE, LIKE, LITERALLY. NO MATTER WHAT QUESTIONABLE CHOICES I'VE MADE OR STUPID RISKS I'VE TAKEN, YOU'VE ALWAYS HAD MY BACK AND MADE SURE I LIVED TO SEE ANOTHER DAY. THANKS FOR THAT. NO REALLY, THANKS." THEN, JOB FELL TO HIS KNEES AND PRAYED THAT GOD FORGIVE HIS FRIENDS FOR BEING JACKASSES AND URGING HIM TO CURSE GOD. HE PRAYED THAT THEY WOULD BE SHOWN MERCY, AND GOD ANSWERED THOSE PRAYERS. HE ALSO BLESSED JOB WITH FORTUNE, FAME, A WHOLE SHIT-TON OF LIVESTOCK, AND MORE DESCENDANTS THAN HE COULD COUNT.

Job 42 LOLV

Lisa Marie Heath

I Did It

As we prepared for graduation everything felt different. Don't get me wrong, I was happy to be able to walk around without a neck brace for a few hours and act 'normal.' Of course, 'normal' also meant going out and drinking at dive bars instead of hanging out with the Dean and other professors on the night before graduation practice. Good thing my head was always killing me, so a little hangover was nothing I wasn't used to. We all made it through practice without issue. Walking across the stage, pausing for a moment at the pulpit positioned at the front of the church where graduation was taking place. God was right, I would be standing up here, and while I may not be speaking to a crowd quite yet, I knew that what I'd accomplished here, was a step in the right direction. That tiny spark of hope nestled in my chest, like the smallest of mustard seeds.

My classmates and I spent the morning chatting with each other about the places we'd traveled together and sharing our plans for the future. I was surrounded by amazing people doing the Lord's work, using their degrees right away before we'd officially graduated. But not me, I was drinking too much, and simply trying to survive day by day. I wasn't yet strong enough to reach out for help. All I had to do was open my mouth, but my pride got the best of me, and I played the part of someone who was excelling in her recovery and excited about the future. I felt like everything had already been stripped from me, so I clung desperately to the little bit of hope I still felt inside from being around my friends.

Before I knew it, the night I'd been waiting for had arrived. In only a few hours I was going to be a master's degree graduate. My parents, Jason, and I all rode to the church together, and we got there early to make sure they could all sit together. The room filled up quickly and, in the hustle, and bustle, I ran into a fellow UCF grad who was receiving her degree as well. It was nice to catch up with her, if even for a moment. My Michael Kors heels were killing me, and while I knew how amazing they looked, I had no idea we would be waiting so long, and I was regretting my decision to not just wear flats. I finally gave up and was one of the first girls to take off their shoes, which started a ripple effect through my classmates.

While we were waiting for the ceremony to begin, I listened as everyone around me was chatting. After being surrounded by my cohort at Southeastern University, I started to recognize that something was off. Without realizing it, my classmates had shown me a piece of myself that had been stripped away after the crash. They were excited, and happy. I was secretly jealous and envious of them all, because I couldn't remember the last time, I'd had a light and carefree conversation. I stood there asking God, "What am I doing here? My life is on a different path now. I don't even know who this 'Lisa' is that they're talking about. It sounds like me, like the me I used to be, but I didn't recognize her anymore. I wanted to cry, to scream. I was damaged, hurt, and scared standing there in the church waiting to receive my degree, and I was wishing that I wasn't alive. My boyfriend was sitting beside my parents, drinking from the flask he'd tucked into his jacket. Mom and Dad were so proud of what their daughter had achieved, they were excited about the future that lay before her. And I couldn't stop thinking about how desperately I wanted to leave the planet. I didn't feel like a leader in Ministry and I sure as flocking hell wasn't going to be using my degree to plant churches. I was torn between being proud of what I'd accomplished and ashamed of the failure I'd become.

Finally, after what seemed like hours, the line started moving and we were able to file into the sanctuary, through the double doors at the back of the church. All eyes were on us, and I put on my mask, smiling from ear to ear, while my mind was screaming at my body not to cry, have a panic attack, or pass out. I made it to my assigned seat, located my parents in the crowd, and took a deep breath, trying desperately to capture this moment. For the next hour we listened as the head of the university spoke as well as a few of my classmates, then it was time. One by one we each crossed the stage, making it official that we were Masters of the Arts in Ministerial Leadership, Church Planting.

As I walked toward the dean, God whispered in my ear. *"Hang on. This part of your journey is just beginning."* I paused, still not quite used to hearing from God at the most inopportune moments, and thought, *"Out of everything you could say to me right now, you chose hang on?"* I'd already taken a gigantic leap of faith. My faith is why I'm still alive today and now you want me to hang on? To what? I shook hands with the dean, accepted my degree and hood, and as I made my way off the stage I locked eyes with my parents, gave them an Elle Woods wink, smile, and mouthed, *"I did it!"*

The night I graduated should have been one of the best nights of my life. But it wasn't. Want to guess what we did after the ceremony ended? That's right, we drank! A lot. The next morning, when we were getting ready to hit the road home, Jason came out of the room with a luggage cart, carrying a cooler full of beer. My dad's face was priceless and ghastly all at the same time. I was humiliated that this was my boyfriend. But what was I supposed to do? What's done was done. We piled into the car and hurried home for a Christmas golf cart parade. If you live in Florida, you understand. The rest of you, trust me, these shindigs are a pretty big deal. After the parade there was going to be a big party at Chad's house to celebrate my graduation and his official housewarming. Everyone was riding around in golf carts and four-wheelers, the alcohol was flowing, and the party kept moving from one house to the next. Chad's bathroom wasn't used to seeing so much action and a plumber had to be called. The entire day was a flocking shit show, and I could keep going but instead, let me break it down into bullet points:

- At some point in the afternoon, Jason's mom asked when I was going to get pregnant. Mind you I was still walking around in a neck brace 90% of the time. *(Eye Roll – LOL)*

- I'd been trying not to wear my brace as much and was shoved out of the way by some jerk. Ouch!
- I met my boyfriend Jason's first sex partner.
- She happened to be the girlfriend of the jerk who'd shoved me.
- I got pissed off, made a scene, and decided I was going to bed.

The thoughts of ending my life were getting worse. Between the depression, alcohol abuse, pot smoking, headaches, black outs, and constant pain, I couldn't handle it anymore. There was no end in sight, and I was devastated that this was my life.

Lisa Marie Heath

BE STRONG. BE BOLD. BE CONFIDENT. AND FEAR NOT BECAUSE YOU'RE NEVER TRULY ALONE, NO MATTER HOW QUIET OR DARK IT MAY SEEM, GOD IS ALWAYS WITH YOU.

Deuteronomy 31:6-8   LOLV

Lisa Marie Heath

Something Was Wrong

On the morning of January 1, 2018, my head was flocking pounding even more than usual. I couldn't seem to get my balance and was barely able to make it from lying in bed to sitting up with my legs on the ground. I was confused, scared, and unable to move. I called out for Jason, asking him to come help, and when he walked into the room, I was shocked to see marks on his arms, chest, and neck.

"Where did you get those marks?" I asked.

"They're from you, Lisa."

"What the hell happened?"

I had no memory of the night before, and because Jason refused to "talk about things that happened in the past," he would never tell me exactly what had transpired. This became a regular occurrence in my life, waking up in the morning with no recollection of what had happened the evening before, and no way of filling in that lost time, because Jason didn't want to talk about it.

Suicide was my only way out from the ringing, all over pain, and having no control over my life. I acted on every impulse, good or bad.

The brain is a very fickle thing. It's the source of all pathways. Something I didn't understand at the time. My brain was holding on for dear life, trying to keep me stable and functioning in order to handle the little amount of people I saw and things that I did. The rest of the time my brain stayed puzzled with what was happening. For all I knew, it was on vacation enjoying not having to work. SMH - LOL I was a shell again with nothing inside besides hatred. People thought they understood the pain, but no one thought of my head. Not even me. Being able to move and function was my first thought. I didn't want to have to rely on anyone but myself to handle the rest. Every time anything negative happened, I would wish to be dead instead of having to deal with it. Overwhelming my brain is a trigger I learned about myself years later, and I'm proud of myself for sticking around to figure it out.

Towards the end of January things between Jason and I were coming to a head. We had a few really rough nights as a couple. I decked his ass, he deserved it, trust me, but the exchange got me banned from a bar. Another night Jason broke down the bathroom door, which I had locked in hopes of getting a few quiet minutes alone. I was officially kicked out of Chad's house after that incident, but that was fine by me. Living at Chad's place with Jason wasn't a good idea for anyone, with it being such a toxic environment. I moved back in with Mom and Dad. I knew that something was seriously wrong with my cognitive reasoning. I was losing time, waking up in places with no idea of how I'd gotten there, and I felt like I'd hit the rockiest of bottoms. To be honest, I did hit rock bottom. I owned nothing but the clothes on my back and my car. I love my parents for not kicking me even further down the spiral. They didn't have to let me move back in at the age of 32. Hospital bills, debit, and student loans drowned me in the hole $200,000.

There were countless occasions where I was told after the fact that I'd been driving people around the night before, with absolutely no recollection of ever being behind the wheel. Talk about scary. At the time, I called these my little blackouts, and because no one else around me seemed concerned about them, I brushed them off as well. My subconscious kept telling me, *"You know this isn't right. You've never wanted to kill yourself. You're not a violent person. This isn't you."* Truly then I didn't realize how big of an impact it made. My mind ran in circles day and night, trying to figure out what was right and wrong in my life.

I'd gotten to a point where my body was in the last stages of healing all 13 fractured bones, and now it was time to focus on what the flock was wrong with me, inside, besides wanting to die every moment of everyday. It didn't ever go away. I was mean, mad, yelling at the world with no clue how I could survive my own thoughts. God was on my hate list for months. I still believed I could prevail, even if I couldn't see the light. My cousin was murdered on Thanksgiving Day 2017, and for the next few months I threw myself into Christmas and New Year's Festivities. His death keeps me alive to this day. At the time though, I wished it would have been me, and not him.

One day after moving back into my childhood home I found some of my old notebooks that my parents had stored in my room. Memory lane was where I was headed. These binders were from the era of the Jabberwocky. The first 3 notebooks/books I pulled out were Counseling Theories, Intro to Clinical Mental Health, and a course book in Behavioral Neuroscience. Then it clicked. With my years spent studying, researching, and writing papers on Neuroscience and Cognitive Behavioral Counseling, I knew what I needed to do. I spent a few days researching the best Cognitive Behavioral Therapists in my area, focusing specifically on those with experience in Post-Traumatic Stress Disorder, Depression, Military Personnel, and a background in Cognitive Behavioral Therapy (CBT). I made phone calls to my top 3 choices and only one was accepting new patients. The receptionist let me know that the earliest open appointment they had was February 14, but that I probably wouldn't want to spend Valentine's Day there in the office. I told her I'd take it. I've never been a huge fan of celebrating Valentine's Day, and it felt serendipitous that I'd be seeing a therapist about a man ruining my life physically, mentally, and financially, that afternoon. After confirming the appointment, I called my best friend at the time and asked if I could come stay with her for a quick break. No, I didn't have the money to make the trip, but that didn't stop me. I knew I needed to get away from Florida, and isn't that what credit cards are for?

When I got back from my brief escape, I was excited about the prospect of meeting with this new therapist, and I prayed that he could provide a little clarity about what was going on inside my head. February 14 finally arrived, and I walked into the therapist's office full of hope and nervous energy. I don't know about you but anytime I walk into a new doctor's office or waiting area, I never know exactly where to look. I was greeted by a girl who asked my last name, *"Heath - H E A T H - like the candy bar."* I rattled off my birthdate and all the other tidbits she needed for this first appointment. I filled out all of the necessary forms and was pretty quickly ushered back to meet Dr. Emeryboard, although he assured me that most of his clients simply called him Dr. E. I asked if we could conduct this first appointment in his office, at the desk, because in reality to me, this was an interview. Before I started spilling my guts and innermost thoughts to this stranger, I wanted to make sure he was going to be the right professional for the job.

For the next 50 minutes I asked every question I could think of regarding the therapy techniques he liked to use, what colleges he attended, where he interned, and how long he'd been practicing. I challenged him by asking if he felt comfortable dealing with clients who mentally fought back. Was he someone who would stand up to me or was he a pushover. I told Dr. E that I needed to work with someone who was raw, real, and didn't sugarcoat shit. Of course, I'd already done a ton of research beforehand, but I wanted to ask my questions face to face to better determine if he was someone I could trust. We agreed that we were a good match, and before I left his office, I warned him that he had his work cut out for him. We parted ways at the reception desk where I scheduled my next few sessions. The first available appointment wasn't for a few weeks, at the beginning of March, but I felt great leaving the office, knowing that I'd just taken a huge step towards figuring out what was wrong with me, and hopefully beginning the process of reclaiming my life. Little did I know that before my first therapy session with Dr. E, I would have entirely new issues to address with him, before we could even begin addressing my past.

What's ironic is that without recognizing it at the time, I alone was responsible for what happened next, the devastation and the clarity. I was still missing time and waking up without any recollection of the day or night before. Asking to die more often than not. I was in constant physical pain from my injuries and the off-beat marching band in my head refused to take a break. I was self-medicating with alcohol and weed, not something I recommend, and Jason and I were fighting more than ever. On this particular day, we were getting along and decided to meet up with our happy hour crew at one of our favorite local bars. Of course, as per usual we started there, and made our way elsewhere to continue the party. I'm not exactly sure when the blackout happened, but by 10pm I was being booked into the local jail.

My memories from that night are spotty at best and have been filled in primarily by others who were there, which means I'm not quite sure how much of it can be trusted. I do remember turning onto a street that connects to the road my parent's house is on. I remember walking to Jason's truck, then being behind the wheel of my mom's truck, and in the blink of an eye, I was handcuffed and sitting behind the metal grate in a police cruiser. My wrists were cuffed behind me, my glasses were sliding down my nose, and out the front window I could see Jason standing beside another patrol car, laughing, and joking with the officers. The next thing I knew, Mom was outside the car, yelling at me through the partially open window, *"Lisa Marie Heath! You don't say a fucking word! Do you want me to take your glasses?"* I leaned towards the window, hanging my head in resignation, and Mom nearly took my ear with her when she ripped my glasses off.

    A few minutes later the sheriff climbed behind the wheel and slammed his door. I tried asking him what had happened. Why was I here? No really, what did I do? *"Shut up! You know good and well what you've done."* Luckily, I knew better than to press the issue, and we drove to the county jail in silence. He parked the car near the back entrance of the building, and before taking me inside, he started typing up his report. I was able to see the screen of his laptop from my position in the backseat and read the details of my arrest as he entered them. *"The assaulted party received scratches on his chest from the detained party."* Scratches? Was I going to jail for scratches? I knew right away that most of those "scratches" had probably come from my *Alex & Ani* bracelets. I loved how pretty they were, with their dangles and charms, but some of those edges were sharp. Hell, I'd scratched myself with them a few times. Besides, I could already feel that my body was covered with scratches and bruises too, they just wouldn't be visible until the next morning. While reading over the officer's shoulder, I noticed that he'd misspelled a word on his report. Thinking he'd want to correct it before sending things to his superior, I mentioned the typo. He told me again to shut up, so I did. Within a few moments his radio buzzed to life. It was his sergeant, letting him know to check the spelling on his report before submitting it again. I remember having to bite my lip to keep from laughing out loud and praying that he wouldn't turn around and see my face.

I've never seen someone's personality change so quickly. The arresting officer turned around in his seat and told me in a much softer tone, *"Because this is your first offense, you'll probably be released on your own recognizance by a judge in the morning. Until then, behave, don't talk back, and you'll be able to spend the night in a holding cell."* As luck would have it though, my experience was nothing like what he'd described. I was arrested a little before 10pm. By 11pm I was being strip searched, given a set of standard issue clothes to change into, and thrown into a holding cell. After what seemed like an hour I was pulled back out of the cell and officially booked. In case you were wondering, my mugshot seriously looks like I was ready to kill someone. It scares me when I look back at it now. By midnight I was being thrown into the general population area and directed to the only open bunk. I can't help but think that I was being treated more like a repeat offender than someone who had just been cuffed for the first time, and over a few scratches no less. Luckily, all the other women in the area were asleep, so I climbed up onto my bunk and prayed for morning.

The next morning, I was led out of the general population area, shackled on both my hands and feet, and stood in front of a judge. It was then that I learned I was being charged with simple domestic battery, and I wasn't alone. There were two other women being charged with the same offense, and the judge made a point of addressing the entire courtroom to say, *"What's wrong with you women? Why are you ladies always beating up and abusing your significant others?"* Because this was my first offense, I was released on a $750 bond, not my own recognizance like the officer had told me. It was noon before the paperwork was completed and Dad was able to bail me out. He'd been at the courthouse as soon as they opened the doors at 9am, cash in hand, but was turned away and told that he'd need to have a check or money order for my bail and wait until everything was completed behind the scenes. Flock!

When Dad and I climbed into his truck, we decided right then and there that we'd be hiring a lawyer. As part of my release, I wasn't allowed to see Jason for 90 days (about 3 months), but as you may have guessed, we were hanging out and drinking together in less than a month. I guess he wasn't *"that"* afraid of me assaulting him. The lawyer we hired was able to have the entire case dismissed and expunged from my otherwise clear record, not only because it was my first offense, but also because there truthfully was no case to begin with. Even with the charges being dropped and expunged, if I were ever to be arrested and charged with assault again, I would more than likely be arrested and sentenced to time in jail. If I laid a hand on Jason again, I was told I'd be spending at least 1 whole year behind bars, no questions asked. Ultimately, that was one of the reasons I knew that I had to move on. Easier said than done. The brain is a very complex system.

My bucket list was getting full of things that I never wanted to do. Remember that therapist? Well, my appointment to get started with him was a few days later.

Great way to start out the session with your mental health therapist. LOL That day I was taught a lesson with a simple technique. Below is the advice that therapist told me:

Look at my options, then STOP.

S- Stop (what's going on?) Figure that out and move on

T- Think (what do I need to do to take control?)

O- Options (what are the choices I can control)

P- Plan what is my plan?? Take three breaths.

He proceeded to say, *"Lisa this can be applied to most situations."* Heck, it couldn't hurt. I mean, I've tried everything else, so I was open to trying to find just one silver lining.

Things continued getting worse and worse by the day, physically, mentally, and emotionally. I was working as a bartender, doing my best to remember people's names, orders, and how to make even the simplest of drinks. The company hired me before my crash. They were the best about letting me come back, even if it was really too early for me to return to work. Cash was needed. While working at the bar, one of my regular customers recommended that I go speak with a lawyer about the crash, because it was obviously still affecting my life and wellbeing. I decided to give it a try, and I met with the lawyer that was on the card the customer gave me. Jason came to the appointment with me, sitting beside me for support while I told the lawyers everything that had happened since the crash, and how I'd been struggling with basic tasks since getting out of the hospital. I signed papers that day, hiring their firm to represent me, with my witness being Jason, someone who would go on to testify against me when everything went to court. If I could go back and do one thing differently in life, it would have been to research my lawyers better, and perhaps meet with a few different firms before signing a contract. I was so trusting at the time, of the people in my daily life as well as strangers. I thought for sure that my new lawyers had my best interests in mind, and that Jason, being there with me, was doing so out of care and concern, not to hear the details of my case and take them back to the opposing side.

While my lawyers did their thing behind the scenes, I continued working at the bar and seeing my therapist 2-3 times a week. Until it was too much. I wasn't able to function anywhere near the level I could before the crash, and eventually I was told that my performance was below where it needed to be. *"You have to ask how to make the simplest drinks. You are great with the customers, but a little flaky when it comes to the rest."* I was humiliated, considering that I was a well-educated, multiple-times graduate, with aspirations of planting and developing a church of her own. Hell prior to the crash, I already had investors ready to send money as soon as I said go. Did I tell you about my plan to create a bar-church? Hear me out, a lot of folks go to church on Sundays but are checking their watches to make sure they're home in time for the game, dying to pop the top on an ice-cold beer. Why not meet them where they'd rather be? I mean, what's wrong with having a drink while you learn the gospel? Anyway, I digress.

I texted my boss explaining everything. He got the message but never returned my call. Once I told my therapist what had happened, we worked on finding skills that I could handle. Allowing us to try and see what type of jobs I could hold down. Within a month or two, we figured it out. I could work for a company in a position doing the same/similar task over and over again. Oh, and something that had medical benefits. So, that's what I did.

Within a month I had been hired and was set to start training in a few weeks. The position I applied for and was offered, was working with cardholders on one of the bank's Visa cards. Woo-hoo! Training consisted of 12 weeks, 4 in a classroom, 4 split between taking a few calls and the classroom, with the last 4 being on the floor taking calls for most of the shift.

The first 4 weeks were spent learning everything about banks and how our bank worked. That was followed by learning about some of our job, ethics, the work environment, all the different training to make sure we're clear on the company policies. Whatever, it was free money to show up and try my best. During the second month of training, while working on the training floor, my back started bothering me really bad. At the time, I honest to God thought the issue was my back. When I went to see my doctor, she told me to go see my OBGYN, and it turns out by working in the position I did, my life was saved. Remember that cancer I had before? Well, it had come back. This time in my left ovary. Surgery was scheduled for November 16th, for a total hysterectomy. Meaning I wouldn't be able to complete my last week of training, and just like that, I was put on medical leave of absence until January of the following year.

Upon returning, the company explained that I would have to go through retraining as well as that the credit card campaign I'd originally been hired for no longer needed staffing. I would be working on the same card team but would be acting as the welcoming committee. I'd be handling entry level questions about the card and working with card holders who had just signed up. It was easier than my first training. After a few hard questions we were able to transfer them to another specialist in a different department with the same card. Makes sense right?? LOL

To say I was ecstatic was an understatement. I was able to be retrained, paid, and earned PTO. Sign me up! It gave me a chance to excel at my job because I would be relearning what I already knew and had a pretty solid idea of what I needed to focus on. It also came with hurdles that I would have to jump over. I now had two different types of therapy with appointments during normal workdays, which wouldn't be an issue if I was working my normal night shifts. Training is only done Monday- Friday 8:30-5:30, the same time as the two other places I needed to be in. How the flock was I going to pull this off?!

It was day 1, I had a list of questions of who to ask about the forms I needed. I'd already learned a little bit from the first round. Meaning figuring out my request for exemptions to allow me the ability to be able to work with my medical issues that were known. When I had the chance between training to be able to fill out and speak to the proper people,

I got in trouble for being late. The thing was if you wanted me to do my job properly, I needed a sit-down stand-up desk, and the ability to leave training to attend my therapies until my normal shift started.

The shit show at Bank of City was a nightmare. No one wanted to help me nor give me the time to get it all taken care of. The departments they wanted me to speak with were only open at the same times as my shift. Ugh. Round and round I went. A month or so later my time off for appointments was being approved so slowly that as the demand of the job got bigger, and the push back for my accommodations got worse, I started drowning in the panic of losing my job on a daily basis. I was good at my actual job. I did have issues they knew about prior, and they'd already agreed to work with me to get the accommodations I needed.

The next month flew by. Trying to juggle everything was a full-time job plus the full-time job at the bank. My brain and body never stopped until I crashed on the weekends. I knew I wasn't going to be able to do this much longer. Then the day came that changed the trajectory of my career. We had now started taking calls on our own before we officially graduated in April. One Friday, I had two back-to-back calls. During the first call, I did not understand what the customer meant. I asked all the questions my brain came up with to be able to transfer him to the right department. Since I did not ask this man for the specific way in which he obtained the message he was calling about, he refused to share with me where he had received this message from the us (our fraud department). I could not do a thing besides try to get him off my phone or transfer. He did it on purpose, something he told me point blank. I kid you not, he actually said, *"You didn't ask the question that way. That's why I didn't answer before."* My blood was boiling. I wanted to say every cuss word I could think of. Instead, my work best friend tried her hardest to help me. She even pulled herself off the phone to put my phone in comment mode. As I transferred the phone picked up a call that fast. Not allowing me time to get myself together with a little break. The next call was with a bank and the customer of the card. The bank wanted to answer all the questions, which is not allowed. It was a process to even get her verified in the system to be able to transfer her where she needed to go. As soon as they answered the questions correctly, I was able to get off the phone. I rushed to take a break, not able to collect myself, and I was sent home early that Friday afternoon.

I was on the phone with my lawyer's assistant as I was coming home from the bank. I was mad, upset, crying, yelling, and freaking out. So much happened in those 30 seconds. The assistant tried to get me to calm down and kept talking. I refused to pull over because if I did, I would never make it home. He kept me from blacking out the whole way home. It was an unhinged moment when nothing else could be done. The next night I woke to realize I had slept for 15 hours straight. Which leads me to one of the lessons I learned from this whole experience, which was:

When working in a high stress job and or call center, I am only able to handle 32 hours max. My last shift of every week was 8 solid hours of HELL. When I hit my limit, I no longer could handle my emotions causing my body to mentally get overwhelmed. As a result, my body would tense up creating an enormous amount of pain. I realized that working 40 hours a week was a trigger for my brain. When overloading, my black outs are created because of the emotions my brain was able to handle/go through, causing me to laugh or cry uncontrollably. Once triggered it would happen randomly over anything. The scariest thing about it all, was that I didn't know how to fix it.

A week went by, and my manager had not pulled me aside. I made it another week. Middle of the work week I got the message I was hoping wouldn't come, even though that's what was going to happen eventually. By the grace of God, I was not fired on the spot after reviewing things with my manager. I was able to continue working until the higher ups reviewed everything and made their decision. For now, though, I still had a job.

Every hoop that Bank of City asked me to complete, I did, just to keep myself employed. It had been a whirlwind of completing every task. Coming up on Memorial Day (weekend). The company approved everything. Now I was just waiting for all departments to review my call to figure out how many rules, regulations, and laws I was breaking. 2 days before the holiday weekend things were slow and I asked if we would be able to get the day off without hurting our good standing, besides receiving no pay. I signed myself up and 30 minutes later I was walking out of work early, headed to my car crying with confusion and conflicting feelings. Should I be happy that I got the day off or scared to walk back into the firing squad? What I can tell you for sure is that I enjoyed that day and a half off.

If you were wondering... Yes, the ringing is still there. Living with head issues and a body that looks healthy but really is a 60-year-old body inside is an unbelievable struggle. The worst part of all though is trying to explain it and having no one believe you. Some days are still worse than others.

Lisa Marie Heath

HEY! GOD HERE. REST EASY AND DON'T FILL YOUR MIND WITH WORRIES ABOUT THE WORLD, THE NEWS, POLITICS, OR WHAT CELEBRITIES ARE STARRING ON THE NEXT SEASON OF DANCING WITH THE STARS. I'M HERE WITH YOU, BESIDE YOU, HOLDING YOUR HAND, AND COMFORTING YOUR EVERY FEAR.

Isaiah 41:10-13 LOLV

Lisa Marie Heath

Hey God, It's Me, Lisa

*I*n a million years I never thought this chapter would start this way, but God had other plans. I'm currently sitting in the exact same place that this part of my story ended.

Bank of City had let me go with good reason, and I immediately started looking for different call center work. Turns out that another major bank was hiring. The whole interview, hiring, and starting process happened fast which was a relief. I hate sitting around doing nothing and had had more than enough of that lately. Training followed behind just as quickly as I'd been hired. I'm proud to say I landed a position within the mortgage department call center and was doubly excited when I found out that my medical benefits kicked in on day one of training. What company does that?! What a blessing. The first 12 weeks were set up as training to learn the systems, rates, processes, and everything else the position required.

I started the job Monday, August 5th, and when I got home that evening, I was feeling like I might be getting sick. I woke up Tuesday morning and my body was aching. As the day progressed, I started feeling weaker and really wasn't sure what was going on. I pushed through with training and took some over the counter meds when I got home in the evening, hoping that a good night's sleep would help. In the middle of the night, I woke up with body shaking chills a serious gut ache, and before I knew it, I was throwing up. By the time Wednesday morning came around it felt like there was an elephant sitting on my chest, but I refused to call out sick from work. I'd just started training 2 days before and convinced myself that I'd caught some stupid stomach bug or infection. I hated the idea of getting anyone else sick, but I knew that something was off about how I was feeling. I knew in my gut that whatever was going on wasn't something I could spread to others. Wednesday and Thursday I felt like death. I had to run to the bathroom to throw up more times than I'd like to admit, not to mention the nearly constant coughing and body cramping in my chest and stomach. I got really good at sneaking out of the training room and closing the door without anyone noticing, running to the shared company bathrooms (sorry to anyone that happened to be in one of the other stalls - no one likes puking in public), and sneaking back into class. Friday was more of the same with the addition of a fever. During lunch that day, one of my coworkers was on the phone with the Human Resource department asking about our new health insurance coverage. We spoke briefly, I figured out which plan I was going to pick, and before I knew it, my new benefits were in place.

    My parents knew how badly I was feeling, so they weren't surprised when I came home from work on Friday and went straight to bed. I told Dad that if I was still feeling this way when I woke up, I'd drive myself to the ER. Well, when I woke up later that night, I grabbed my bag and headed for the Emergency Room. My visit was short. I explained all my symptoms, the vomiting, the stomach cramping, and worst of all, the fact that I was struggling to breathe, but instead of taking a minute to listen to the patient, the on-call doctor preformed one tested, a urinalysis. That's it. While we were waiting for the results, a nurse brought me some pain meds and once it was decided that the only thing wrong with me was a UTI, they sent me home with a prescription for antibiotics.

When I got back to the house, I told Dad what had happened, that I was going to try to get a few more hours of sleep, and when I woke back up, I'd go to a different hospital, because there was absolutely no way that a UTI was causing me to have issues with trying to breathe. I managed to sleep through the entire day, and night, not waking up until Sunday morning when my cell phone started buzzing beside me. I answered the phone and told my friend Heather that yes, I had been sleeping since I'd gotten home from hospital #1 the previous morning. She ordered me to get dressed because she was coming to pick me up and take me to a different ER. When Heather got to the house, she helped me pack an overnight bag, picked me up in her arms, carried me through the house and settled me into the passenger seat of her car. Dad held open the house door as Heather and I left, and as we passed, I told him I loved him. I'm sure that was unsettling for him, and Heather scolded me for it when she got in the car. 15 minutes later we were parked in front of the Emergency Room entrance. Heather found a wheelchair, lifted me into it, and slowly pushed me into the hospital. It was no more than a minute or two before I was being prepped for an x-ray of my chest.

Have you ever seen an x-ray of someone with pneumonia? How about an x-ray for someone who died from pneumonia? Well, spoiler, they're pretty shocking images. Within minutes I was being asked which hospital I'd prefer to be admitted to.

Heather left the Emergency Room and went to the house to pick Mom up so they could both meet me at the hospital. I remember bits and pieces of them getting me situated in a room, but then, everything goes black.

I remember being moved into an ambulance for the drive to the hospital. As I was being wheeled into a room, I told Heather and Mom all about how one of the paramedics looked exactly like Chandler Bing from Friends. We laughed and told the guys thank you for all of their help in getting me from the ER to my new room safely, as well as for putting up with my crazy antics. I'm still not sure how Heather and Mom beat me to the hospital since I was riding in style in an ambulance. I remember Heather or Mom handing me the eye mask I wear to sleep. And that was it. Everything went black for the next 2 weeks.

I don't remember those two weeks in the hospital. It took reading messages and talking with friends and family for me to piece together what happened during that lost time. It was hard for me to hear their stories. Some of them still don't talk about that time.

While my friends and family were praying for a miracle from beside my bed, my body, I was already above them. I was watching myself sleep. It's the weirdest thing to try explaining to people, the idea of opening your eyes and seeing yourself sleeping. I still shake my head every time I think about it. Some people will tell you that they've been to heaven, seen the angels, and been drawn toward a bright light at the end of a hallway. For me, it all looked familiar. And, at the same time I didn't pay much attention to my surroundings. I mean, who wants to focus on the color of the wallpaper when you're standing face to face with God?

"Hey Lisa. Good to see you again."

"God, why am I here? I've got so many questions."

"Well, you've got a choice to make."

"Umm, no."

"You were just looking down at your own body Lisa. What did you see?"

"Is this a trick question? I saw myself sleeping with a few people sitting around my bed."

"You sure?"

"Well shit. Now I for flocking sake am not."

"Look again."

At that moment I looked back down at my body, lying lifeless in the hospital bed, hooked up to so many different machines. Turning around, I yelled at God.

"What the Hell is going on God???"

"Actually, never mind, why me? Why my family? Why again??"

"Lisa, I know how stubborn and determined you are. You always have so many questions, but I'm only going to answer one."

"Why am I here with you?"

He paused.

Now, when I say God, I'm talking about my higher power. He made us in his eyes so we could see him how he wanted us to. We're all created differently and believe in many different things. I love that about Him.

"You're here, and your body is there."

"God, I can see that."

"Well, you get a choice to stay here with us or stay alive for many more years to come. But you need to make your choice soon."

God just looked at me. Sure, he gave us freewill, but he already knew what I was going to choose.

At the same exact moment, we nodded to each other, and I heard a voice yelling out "*WEEEIIISSSAAAA.*" I had tears in my eyes as I turned to see my cousin Logan, rushing towards me, picking me up, and swinging me around. Finally, he set me back down on my feet and gave me the biggest bear hug.

Just like that, it all came flooding back. The moment I'd heard he was gone. The moment I learned that he, my baby cousin, had been murdered. Hearing that news only a month after having my own crash, caused me to question if I was better off dead because of the pain I felt in my heart from losing him, and the bone piercing physical pain in my own body from the waist up.

Snapping back, Logan asked how the family was doing, his mom, brother, sister and niece. As a whole we were doing great. I told him that each of us were grieving him differently. I asked if he'd seen that his mother was diagnosed with an actual broken heart. Looking down, he cried and told me that yes, he he'd seen everything, and tried to show her that he was okay in every way he could.

"Logan, my sweet cousin, we know you're okay. But living without you is like dying as well."

Logan hugged me tight and as he held me; I could hear my grandmother calling my name.

"Lisa Marie."

"Grandma Ruby," I yelled while reaching my arms out to hug her.

"Oh, Lisa. I'm so proud of you. What an amazing woman you have turned out to be. So much like my son. Look who was right! That would be me!" she said, pointing to herself. I knew exactly what she was talking about.

"Yes! Yes! Yes! Grandma, I went to COLLEGE! And my high school grades didn't matter at all since I transferred to a university from a state college!!"

I stuck my tongue out at her.

"Either way, God made it work."

Right.

"Hey God."

"Yes Lisa?"

"Why was my path to finish up with an M.A. in Ministerial Leadership and Church Planting?"

"You think I am going to tell you why I made sure you graduated? You know me better than that." Stated God.

"Ok, then can you at least share a little insight into why my life feels so much like Job's?"

Instead, of answering, God asked if I was ready to make my choice.

"You can stay here if you like, or you can go back. That's free will."

"How long do I have to make my decision? It's a pretty big one after all."

"The decision needs to be made Lisa. Your body can't hold on without you for long. But I have an idea of something that might help you."

I knew when I turned around that I would see Chris, my fiancé, walking toward me. Well played Sir, well played God.

I stopped Chris before he could get too close to me. I knew that if I hugged him once, I would have to stay there with him. There was no doubt in my mind. I missed my best friend that much. As tears were running down my face, Chris smirked and asked, *"So, what you going to do?"*

"Hi to you too slacker. Chris…"

"Lisa, stop. It happened. I am here, and you are here. But you can't stay. Not yet. I won't let you. The world needs you in it. They just aren't ready. We'll all be up here, fighting the battle in the background. Lisa, you're stronger than any Marine I know. Hoo-Rah!

Logan chimed in, "Once a Marine always a Marine."

I looked at Chris, my grandma, Logan then again back to Chris.

"Lisa, you know in your heart that it's not your time yet. You've survived losing me and so many other people in your life. Other people die of broken hearts, they hold on to past resentments, and they give up, but not you. You need to teach people how to forgive, how to move on, and be alive. I'm always going to be here for you, we all are. You're never alone, you have Arc Angel Michael, Apollo, and the rest of us as your guardian angels, always surrounding you. When you walk into a room people stare because they can see your light, and the world right now is a very dark place."

"But Chris, it isn't fair."

"Life isn't fair Lisa, but you have to keep going, no matter how hard it gets. You need to make your decision. Right before you arrived, the doctors told you that to save your life, your lungs needed a break. Without hesitating you said yes, then looked at your dad and mom. Within an hour, you were intubated and placed on full oxygen. You haven't been breathing on your own. Doctors are at a loss as to what to do next. You know who needs you more. Plus, you know we aren't going anywhere.

"Go back and wake up. You've been on life support Lisa and the doctors are telling your mom and Dad that they need to prepare to say goodbye. They're sitting beside your bed, holding your hands, and pouring their hearts out to you, begging for you to fight for your life."

"I love you, Chris. I miss you."

"I love you too, Lisa, and I don't expect to be seeing you again anytime soon."

"Alright God, I'm ready to go back. I hate you, but you have a plan."

God told Michael that I was ready to go back. And, just like that I was back in my body. Wondering what was going on? Why can't I speak? Are my hands cuffed to the bed? Where am I?

Fast forward 4 days and I was finally leaving the hospital after two and a half weeks. There was a single nurse that rushed over to give me a hug and tell me that she was so relieved to see me going home. She'd been the first person to intubate me, and at the time, it wasn't expected for me to leave the room unless it was in a body bag.

I would find out later that I'd been intubated numerous times, as well as being on a ventilator for 5 full days. I was moved in and out of the ICU because I would wake up, then black out again. When one of the doctors was checking on me, he asked if there was anything that I'd been doing lately that could have affected my lungs. Jason was there visiting at the time and proceeded to pull my vape pen out of the side pocket of my purse. The doctor immediately told Jason and my parents that the issue could be a combination of the non-dispensary grade marijuana in my vape pen and/or the battery that is used to heat it up. I was one of the very first cases of chemical pneumonia related to vaping, so the doctors and nurses were trying everything they could to save me, but much of my treatment was trial and error. At some point, my oncologist was called in, because the cancer in my ovaries had been mesothelioma and the fear was that it may have come back and spread to my lungs.

While lying in the ICU with a tube down my throat and my wrists bound to the bed, I was terrified that I'd been admitted to the psych ward. I found out later that it had just been a precaution, so that if I did wake up, I wouldn't be able to rip the tubes out of my mouth. I remember a nurse talking about the treatments they were going to give me, now that I was awake. I kept trying to get out a message to them, that I was feeling smothered and trapped. They had me try and write out what I was wanting to say. Do you know how hard it is to try spelling 'claustrophobic?' I tried desperately to communicate what I was feeling, but later learned that I was writing letter after letter on top of each other, fully unable to communicate. I was frustrated, angry, and threw the dry erase marker at the nurse.

Flock, that was not a good idea. She asked everyone to leave the room, and once we were alone, she had a come to Jesus meeting with me. She informed me how things were going to be, and I locked eyes with her, letting her know silently that I understood. She told me that the doctor would be coming by to explain what was going on, as well as to take the tubes out because I was not getting the right levels of oxygen. I shook my head in agreement. Later that day the tubes finally came out, and I immediately started asking the doctor when I could go home.

He told me that the answer was a definite NO, that I would have to sign a waiver stating that I was leaving against doctor's orders. I told him to get me the paperwork!

"Why am I here at the hospital anyway?"

"You don't know?"

"No. That's why I wanted to see you."

"Well, you had pneumonia."

"That's it? Let me have that paperwork, I want to go home."

The doctor left the room and when his assistant game back he scolded me for how I was speaking to the doctor. That was the last time I gave the hospital staff a piece of my mine. I told the assistant that neither he nor the doctor were welcome in my room again.

When my parents came back to my room after eating dinner, I was extremely emotional over how I'd been treated. The nurse who I now loved on day shift asked me if she could help brighten my spirits in any way and I told her that I really just wanted to see my baby (puppy) Allie Mae. She told me that if she could help us sneak her in, she would, and we laughed telling her that she'd be caught right away. I love my princess but man, the beagle in her would cause one heck of a situation in the hospital. While we were talking about my dog, I showed the nurse the little stuffed dog that hadn't left my side. It was the closest looking pup that Jason could find and had helped keep me company until I'd be able to see Allie Mae. Later in the day, the ICU nurse tried to lift my spirits again by showing me the handsome men working on the roof of the building next to us. Dad laughed, telling her that my mom and I had already been checking them out all week. LOL

Knowing that having children would be hard, and the fact that my mother cursed me; telling the universe that if I ever had children of my own, she wished them to be 10 times worse than I was, my animals became my children. Allie Mae Heath came into my life when we both needed each other's strength to keep going. We are both fighters in this world. The love I have for my 10-year daughter can be summed up by the saying I have hanging over our bed at home. "I choose you. And I'll chose you, over, and over, and over. Without pause, without a doubt, in a heartbeat. I'll keep choosing you Allie." I love you, big girl. Even though you'll never read this. Everyone else will know.

The staff were shifting from the day to night crew, and the overnight nurse was one that had been on my case for a few nights, so I begged my mother to go home and sleep. She had aged 5 years in 2 weeks, and I knew that she desperately needed her rest. Plus, I was alive and breathing better. Dad and I finally got her to leave.

It was my first night alone and I was finally able to start processing everything the doctors had told me. A few hours later I asked the nurse if she knew where my phone was. She found it in the closet, under a blanket or pillow, and when I woke up the screen, I saw more notifications than I thought were possible. After spending a week 'with God' I now had the pleasure of trying to figure out what I had been talking about with the people in my life. The pictures and messages, waiting on my phone made me realize that all of these people, they didn't even know where I was, or what was going on. Not even my best friend at the time. There's no room for that story in this book, but it will be told someday.

My dad did his absolute best, trying to let my closest friends know about my situation, but at the end of the day he was most worried about his daughter trying to fight for her life. The nurse came in with my 4-hour doses of medication and breathing treatment, tiptoeing to not wake me if I was finally getting some sleep. She was so sweet, and actually managed to place my breathing treatment on my face while I slept one night, just to keep from waking me.

The next day, I was finally told what had actually been going on. All the details from the beginning. It started with my being placed on a ventilator to try and give my lungs a chance to heal. I was told that at that point it was the only option left before I physically died. The doctors couldn't believe how in tune I was to my body's needs and the fact that I wanted to be at home recovering. It was decided that if all of the different departments would sign off on my being discharged, I could plan on being home in just a few days.

Later that day I was moved out of the ICU and back into a pressurized room, where I could be kept from developing any other infections in my lungs while they continued to heal. This room had a view of the Helipad which was amazing. I know it sounds odd, but I grew up right outside a military base, so the sounds of jets, airplanes and helicopters are soothing to me. I feel at home seeing them and being able to hear them taking off. After dying, seeing the hope of rescue-taking actions warmed my heart. Each time I said a prayer for everyone involved. I was reminded of one of my ambitions, to be a Chaplin in the Navy, stationed overseas. Being someone that gave people hope and comfort in times of struggle. It was the least I could do in those moments when the helicopter landed or took off. While discussing this chapter with my editor via Zoom, there were countless aircraft passing overhead. I get it God; I'm doing what I'm meant to.

The next specialist to visit was my Mesothelioma doctor. He had been called in to help when they were having a difficult time trying to figure out what to do. I was so worried that my crazy cancer had made its way to affecting my lungs, but luckily, I was *only* dealing with Chemical Pneumonia, from the battery that heated up the liquid in my vaping marijuana device. What in the world???? I'd never heard of this happening, although I wasn't surprised when they said that was the issue. I lived with my vape pen the entire time I was recovering from the crash. Literally, I carried it in my sports bra, bathing top, or very close to me at all times.

They ordered more x-rays, a CT scan, swallow, and respiratory tests. After the doctors left, at some point my parents showed back up to the hospital. I told them what all the doctors said, and that my hope was to go home in 3 days. My dad looked at me in a crazy way.

"You are not coming home until the doctors say so. You were just dead. Relax, Allie is fine. She's been with Jason the whole time."

I was so excited for the swallowing test. It meant I could finally try to chew. What can I say, it had been a while and it's the little things in life we so often forget to be thankful for. Those everyday automatic functions the body naturally does for us. I can't even recall having the x-ray because of my excitement over the swallowing test. It might also have something to do with my adventure of getting in the chair to do the exam.

The nurse who was tasked with transporting me from my room to the waiting room for the exam asked me if I could stand and get in the wheelchair, she had ready for me. I told her, of course I can do that. She helped me sit up in bed, then swivel to put both feet on the floor, and holding my hands, helped stand me up slowly. Once my feet hit the floor it felt so good to touch the cool tile, especially after 2 weeks of nothing by lying in a hospital bed. Of course, no sooner had I realized I was standing up, than my body gave up and I was falling to the floor.

We were both caught off guard and the nurse asked me, *"When was the last time you stood up?"* I told her that it had been 2 weeks.

"Well, no wonder you don't have any strength! You haven't used your muscles in weeks! Let me go get us some help."

Why on God's green earth did I think I could stand up, let alone walk, without issues. While she was finding someone to help us, I realized that I was literally skin and bones. All my muscles had withered away. Not only did I die, but my body was also dying. I was a skeleton.

During the swallowing test, the doctor made sure that nothing had happen to my trachea when I'd been intubated or hooked up to the ventilator. Luckily, my swallowing functions were normal, much better than the muscles in my legs. The doctor gave me a few textured foods and soft chewing foods as well to watch me eat. The process was totally cool. My neck was behind an X-ray machine. She watched the whole time, while I had a piece of food in my mouth and throat. I distinctly remember that one of the samples she provided was cinnamon graham crackers. It tasted great but I was starving for real food. We got done and I was off to the room again. It felt like I was Dorothy from the Wizard of Oz, off to see the Wizard. I was unaware that in reality, I was the wizard. It's very fitting, I think.

Jason told my parents the day before that he would stay the night with me at the hospital and as soon as I was cleared to eat real food, I called him up.

"Hey!! I want my normal from Panera please."

Jason was good to my family while I was in the hospital. That night he explained that many of them had switched off staying with me each night. Holding my hand while putting my light-blocking eye mask on. I flipped through channels on the TV, we talked, and he showed me pictures of my Allie Mae. He loved her too and knew that if something were to happen to her, I would have to be restrained in the psych ward. He was a good man, when he wasn't drinking. I will give him that. I found something on TV that I could fall asleep to. It was a movie Jason had never seen. I tried explaining the characters and story plot to him but eventually we both gave up and fell asleep.

During the night, the nurse came in several times. Each time I was wide awake doing something on my phone or staring out the window. She asked if I was in pain, and I told her that I wasn't. I just couldn't sleep. My body had rested for 2 weeks, and I was ready to go home. She told me that I was doing remarkable given my situation, that I was beating the odds and recovering faster than the doctors could have expected. I winked at her.

"It's because I've already been healed. My body is just weak. God sent me back down for a reason. I'm blessed to be here getting a chance to show people how a real relationship with God can be."

She smiled, and I smiled back. At that moment she noticed my central line on my left arm.

"Has this been changed since you woke up Lisa?"

"No ma'am, not to my knowledge."

She left the room and came back with a new central line kit, and while she was trying to get things changed in the day without hurting me, Jason woke up. He asked if she might have better luck with the lights on, and after giving us a second to brace ourselves for the offensive fluorescent light, she turned them on and saw that my arm had become infected. She cleaned things up and decided to let my arm breathe to heal. I still have a scan from the port hole, and a line where the infection was. Another reminder of how lucky I am.

After she finished with my arm I crashed until the doctors came by the next morning. I really liked my infectious disease doctor, he and the other specialists worked well together. He told me all the test were coming back with good signs, but it would still be at least another day before I was able to go home. I still needed approval from the respiratory specialist.

Before I knew it Jason was leaving for the day and my parents were on their way. I was disappointed that I wasn't going home but was excited, knowing that it was happening soon. I felt like I was in jail. LOL. That day took forever too. Each hour felt like four. I watched my mother nap. My Uncle and Aunt came to visit. My uncle Jerry was funny. He told me he knew that I was starting to feel like myself again because when he walked into the room, I'd flipped him off. Oh, Jerry, I just love you. Our bond is different, but I wouldn't trade any of it for the world. He understood me more than anyone else during my recovery. He too had a hard time catching his breath.

I sent everyone home early. There was nothing they could do, and I was just waiting for my final breathing treatment which was hours away. I also knew Jason would be up to my room at some point, and just as I predicted he was, right after he got off work. That night I stared out my window thinking back to Chris. I missed him so much more now. Jason was just a friend to me at that point and I wanted the bear hug that I'd had to leave heaven without getting. I cried thinking of him. Knowing that it was going to be a very long time before I would see him again.

That next morning the doctor came in for a minute to tell me that I would finally be doing my respiratory test, and maybe even getting to go home. I screamed a little.

"You're not joking right?"

"No Lisa. You're doing really well. I just want to make sure your lungs are strong enough to go home."

"I totally understand. I do not want to see you in this hospital again. Your office yes, but anywhere but here."

Later that morning, I remember seeing a pair of black scrubs, which in Florida, are worn by folks in the respiratory department. He was cute too. He helped me up and ran me through a few small actions to see how my breathing was. I kept running out of breath, which was crazy. From being a half-marathon runner to barely being able to move from side to side without taking a break. He let me catch my breath before the big test, walking around the entire floor. But I was ready. I would be pushing myself physically for the first time since being wheeled in. We walked and stopped, walked and stopped. It was flocking hard. My levels were all over the place. I told him as we were walking that I really wanted to leave, and he said that I was doing good for my real first walk.

I was released later that day. Free at last and headed home to see my Allie Mae. That night would be the last time Jason stayed with me. He chose alcohol over our friendship. Because I was back home, he assumed that I was okay. Far from it. Until now, I have never really discussed what the final straw for Jason and I was, but Chris was right. I was here for a purpose that had nothing to do with the people who didn't really want to stay in my life. It's a hard process to grasp. Some connections are harder to let go of than others. One piece of advice for all of us though, if they're not pushing you to be your best self, are they really your friends?

Remember earlier in this chapter when I said that I was here for many reasons? Well, one of them was to contact my local new station to share with them my story, to warn others of the dangers of vaping. I sent an email a few days after I came home. At that time my city was under a tropical storm warning, and all the local stations were sharing minute by minute updates on the storm. As soon as we were out of danger though, I received a response, asking me if I would be okay with doing an interview. I said, "yes." They told me that they'd love to come by and meet with me ASAP, to run a report on my case that evening.

I agreed and a few hours later they were showing up at my house mic'ing me up and talking me through how the interview would work. Let me be totally honest, I was a nervous wreck. I didn't want to say the wrong thing and the best part of the interview was watching it live with my doctor backing up what happened. That was the beginning of me telling the world; You're not ready for my sparkle!

Lisa Marie Heath

Here We Are Now

As I sit here at my desk, reflecting on the stories I've just shared, the scars I've shown, and the confessions I've made, I'm reminded of how precious life is, no matter how tumultuous or crazy it may seem at times. And I DO NOT want you closing this book, thinking, *"Wow, what a shit life Lisa's had."* No, no, no, no, no! I want you to finish reading these pages and walk away with a newfound or newly strengthened understanding of what a genuine and authentic relationship with God can look like. Sure, my life is very much like that of Job, in that we were both given struggle after struggle, seemingly in hopes of breaking our faith. But at the end of the day, or in this case, the end of the book, what matters most is keeping faith. Talking to God, whether that be in a church, your car, or while you're on the pot. Just keep that conversation going and check in every so often to share the good and the bad, your excitement, accomplishments, and cries for help. Maybe don't curse at him quite as much as I do though. I mean, it's completely up to you, the language you use when chatting with your higher power, but I'm definitely trying to work on not screaming expletives in his direction quite as much these days.

Personally, I continue to have faith in God because I've seen time and time again that if I didn't have my faith, I wouldn't be here. My faith is what holds me here. I still don't know what God's plans for me are. But I do know that I trust him. I have faith that Gods plan will be just as it's meant to be, and when the time is right, he'll let me in on that secret. What I do know is that I'm here to speak. My God-given purpose is to talk about the things that I've gone through and still go through. The good, the bad, and the really really ugly. Because we as a community desperately need to actually understand God and the universe.

Now, in case you've been skimming through these pages, or if you're one of those people who skip to the last chapter to see how the story ends *(spoiler: this is NOT the end of my story)*, here's a quick recap for you:

- I graduated from high school in May 2004.

- I was first diagnosed with cancer in 2006.

- I went to Cosmetology School & became a Cosmetologist later in 2006.

- My finance passed away in August of 2008.

- I graduated from Florida State College of Jacksonville in August 2010.

- Following Junior College, I attended and proudly became an alma mater of University of Central Florida in December 2012.

- The crash that completely changed my life was in October 2017.

- I graduated from Southeastern University on December 15, 2017.

- I was diagnosed with cancer again in 2019, which lead to my full hysterectomy at the age of 34.

- I started my first business from the comfort of my bed while recovering from Chemical Pneumonia in September of 2019.

- In 2020, I decided to hire my first personal development coach, and invest in myself, my professional development, and finally put all of my fancy degrees to good use by sharing my story and voice with the world.

- In October of 2022, I took a gamble and attended a mastermind. It was a huge investment and one that changed my life, discovering how all of my past education combined to support my bigger purpose.

- In November of 2022, I hired a professional editor, and now, less than a full year later, I'm proud, petrified, and excited beyond flocking belief to claim the status of Author.

Are you ready for some crazy coincidences?

- Chris, my fiancé, passed away on August 16, 2008, fast forward to the same day in 2019, when I was placed on the life support.

- Aug 21, 2008, I was able to spend a few hours with Chris at the funeral home after his body was brought back home to Florida. The same day, 11 years later, I was able to breathe on my own without a ventilator after visiting Chris in heaven.

· August 23, 2008, we laid Chris to rest, and August 23, 2019, I was released from the hospital.

Writing this book has been... well, therapeutic. It's been an experience. It was a struggle, a release, and it's been healing. The process of revisiting memories, experiences, and feelings that I've done my best to hide away has been eye-opening and inspiring. Taking a closer look not only at the trials I've overcome, but the ways in which I've survived and thrived in a world where so often it felt easier to give up, give in, and fade away. My relationship with my parents is stronger than ever, although we still bicker on occasion, they can be old and crotchety sometimes, but I wouldn't trade their love for anything in the world. I may not be wealthy, famous, or recognized as a household name (yet), but I'm genuinely happy. Every day I wake up with the drive to create the life that I desire and inspire others to see their own lives as being worthy and deserving of happiness and love.

What happens next is anyone's guess. Although I know that God already has plans in the works for me, and my faith is in the Lord.

Until we meet again.

xoxo

Lisa Marie Heath

Epilogue

What if you woke up one day to find out that the pathways in your brain had been hit? Now, for the rest of your life, those paths are forever gone. What would you do? How would you feel if something was wrong, but you couldn't express it without frustration? With none of the words coming out right? Having gaps of time and spaces that disappeared. What about when negative thoughts overrun your brain from reality?

In December of 2019, I was being deposed for the first time in relation to the crash I shared about earlier. That day was one of the worst days I've had. 45 minutes into the interview my lawyer stopped everything. Asking for a break, he gave me time to rest and rebalance. My emotions were all over the place, as they should be, reliving that day and everything that happened. When my brain heard the word "MRI," I had a mini heart attack. That was a huge trigger for me, because of the pain I experienced, and the noise the machine made. To this day, just hearing the word gives me a physical twitch. The lawyers told me to go home and rest. Resting was a must, however, my lawyer left me with one last intriguing question. *"Do you have a PBA?"* When I didn't respond, he asked me again, and I still didn't have a clue what he meant by a PBA. I responded, *"Umm, I don't know. Why?"* That's when he told me we were going to stop the interview. As soon as I got home, I had my computer open, and I was looking up what the heck a PBA was.

Pseudobulbar Affect. PBA. It's a medical condition that causes involuntary, sudden, and frequent episodes of crying and/or laughing in people living with certain neurologic conditions or brain injuries. Well looks like I needed to find a new neurologist. It was the week of Christmas. No one was open, which left me with plenty of time to keep researching at home. After the new year, I called a few offices, asking to talk with the best neurologists in North Florida. I was not in the mood to play around. It took me a whole year to be seen by someone, for multiple reasons, most of which were insurance and job-related.

Then, on February 4, 2020, I met with Dr A, a top neurologist in the area. My brain was going to be pushed full throttle. I became a human lab rat, and I was in no way prepared for the work it was going to take to retrain my brain and the side effects that I would experience throughout the process. But that, my friends, is a story for another day.

About The Author

Lisa Heath is a fiercely fabulous author, public speaker, founder of Life of Lisa Inc & HEATH Foundation, as well as an advocate for individuals living with TBI's & their caregivers. For more information about Lisa's story, additional titles & how you can book Lisa for your next event, visit her website at www.lifeoflisaheath.com.

www.ingramcontent.com/pod-product-compliance
Lightning Source LLC
Chambersburg PA
CBHW050731010526
44107CB00010B/814